© Editorial Gustavo Gili, SA, Barcelona, 1999

Impreso en España
ISBN: 1-58423-019-3
Depósito legal: B. 7.664-1999

Published in the United States of America, 1999
GINGKO PRESS Inc.

Time architecture brings together sixteen projects in which the temporal factor is as important as the spatial, the obvious basis of all construction. In these works, however, 'temporal' is not necessarily synonymous with 'ephemeral'. In fact Enric Miralles and Benedetta Tagliabue believe less in a conception whose meaning is directed towards a final closure than in an ongoing work made up of instants in which, as Goethe remarked to Eckermann, each step along the way is, without ceasing to be a step, a goal in itself. Between space, time and movement, these architectures bear witness to a journey which extends from exhibitions in Harvard, Venice and Copenhagen to the Contemporary Art Fair in Madrid, taking in the play of shadows a building produces, the design of elements destined for other, childhood, games, and the changing set design of an opera premièred in the architects' own Barcelona studio. The projects presented here combine architectural reality with its representation to create a new reality that enables a constructed and essentially immovable space to move –in time– from continent to continent. Thanks to their migratory nature these works are consistently different without, for all that, ceasing to be themselves.

Arquitecturas del tiempo reúne dieciséis proyectos en los que el carácter temporal es tan importante como el espacial, fundamento evidente de toda construcción. Sin embargo, en estos trabajos, temporal no es necesariamente sinónimo de efímero. De hecho, Enric Miralles y Benedetta Tagliabue creen menos en un planteamiento cuyo sentido se encamina a un final cerrado que en una obra en marcha hecha de instantes en la que, como recordaba Goethe a Eckermann, cada paso es una meta sin dejar de ser un paso. Entre espacio, tiempo y movimiento, estas arquitecturas testimonian el viaje que va de las exposiciones en Harvard, Venecia o Copenhague a la Feria de Arte Contemporáneo en Madrid, pasando por el juego de sombras que produce un edificio, el diseño de elementos destinados a otros juegos, los infantiles, o la escenografía cambiante de una ópera estrenada en el estudio barcelonés de los propios arquitectos. Los proyectos aquí presentados entremezclan la realidad arquitectónica con su representación para crear una realidad nueva que permite mover de continente en continente –a través del tiempo– un espacio construido y en principio inamovible. Merced a su carácter viajero, estas obras son siempre diferentes, sin dejar nunca de ser las mismas.

The Venice Biennale
Venezia. 1996
Mies van der Rohe Pavilion
Barcelona. 1997
The Nordic Tour
Århus, Stockholm, Copenhague. 1998
Graduate School of Design
Harvard. 1993

Miralles **Tour**

The exhibitions that have presented the work of Enric Miralles and Benedetta Tagliabue in different countries constitute a personal invitation to the voyage: each city has seen a similar show recreated in a different montage. Aside from being projects in themselves, each exhibition forms a sort of changing, portable anthology of their architecture. It could be said that these projects inject lightness and movement into the solidity of the built edifice at the same time as they create a journey through space, from continent to continent, which arrests and takes the measure, at least for an instant, of the passing of time. "There are," said Lichtenberg, "two ways of prolonging life. The first consists in putting the maximum distance between the two points of birth and death, and thereby extending the journey. So many machines and objects have been invented for extending the journey that, were one to limit oneself to merely observing them, it could be hard to believe that they serve for making the journey any longer; some doctors have made great advances in this field. The other way consists in walking more slowly, leaving the two points where God desires them to be; this is the way of the philosophers, who have discovered that the best thing is to walk in a zigzag, botanizing and trying to jump a ditch here, and further on, where the ground is bare and nobody sees them, performing a somersault."
From Boston to Venice and from north to south, these projects give an account of the lingering and steadfast journey of the architect, who comes and goes without taking his projects to be complete and, at the same time, without ceasing to advance.

Miralles **Tour**

Las exposiciones que han dado a conocer la obra de Enric Miralles y Benedetta Tagliabue en diferentes países constituyen una particular invitación al viaje: cada ciudad ha visto una muestra similar recreada en un montaje diferente. Amén de ser proyectos en sí mismos, cada exposición constituye una suerte de antología mutable y portátil de su arquitectura. Se diría que estos proyectos inyectan levedad y movimiento a la consistencia de los edificios construidos, a la vez que crean un periplo en el espacio, de continente a continente, que mide y detiene, siquiera un instante, el paso del tiempo. "Hay" –escribe Lichtenberg– "dos vías para prolongar la vida. La primera consiste en distanciar al máximo uno de otro los dos puntos, el del nacimiento y el de la muerte, alargando así el camino. Para alargar este camino se han inventado tantas máquinas y objetos que, si uno se limitara sólo a verlos, difícilmente podría creer que sirvan para hacer más largo un camino; algunos médicos han hecho grandes avances en este campo. La otra vía consiste en caminar más lentamente, dejando los dos puntos extremos donde Dios quiere que estén; es la vía de los filósofos, quienes han descubierto que lo mejor es caminar en zigzag, herborizando e intentando saltar aquí un foso y, más allá, donde el terreno esté limpio y nadie los vea, dar una voltereta".
De Boston a Venecia y del sur al norte, estos proyectos dan cuenta del camino demorado y firme del arquitecto, que va y viene sobre sus proyectos sin darlos por acabados y, a la vez, sin dejar de avanzar.

The Venice Biennale '96

Biennale Architecture section Director/
Director de la sección Arquitectura de la Bienal: Hans Hollein
Architects/**Arquitectos:** Enric Miralles & Benedetta Tagliabue
Collaborators/**Colaboradores:** Elena Rocchi, Miquel Lluch,
Fabián Asunción, Pep Villar, Germán Zambrana, Piercarlo Comacchio
Photographs/**Fotografías:** Domi Mora, Giovanni Zanzi
Oil Paintings/**Óleos:** Roger Páez

Invited by Hans Hollein to intervene in the Venice Biennale on the theme of 'Sensors of the Future: The Architect as Seismograph', Miralles and Tagliabue responded by proposing a montage that would collate the various phases and different designs contained in their project for the Huesca Sports Palace (1988-94). "It seems," observe the architects, "that he who speaks last is right. It appears that the latest building is the only one that can be spoken of. For this reason it's difficult to make a leap forward in time and act as sensors of the future. Our solution is to always say the same thing, or almost the same. We propose small variations in a work which does not take it that the building has a sense of finality, a temporal status, but which believes, rather, that a project is made up of unconnected instants, which communicate things that are independent of each other, which are superimposed... but which appear equal. At times only the person who's capable of consistently stating and making the same movement seems to advance. This small vibration may say something about the future."

Their intervention, which received the Leone di Oro award, consisted of a maquette of the first version (as a first anticipation of seeing the completed building); a circular diorama which provided a totalizing vision of the Palace - inside, outside and above - from within that particular magic ring; a triptych in oil which represented the interior details on a scale of 1:1; a photographic alphabet of letters formed by the building's shadows; various photos of the town of Huesca; and a black-and-white photomontage in which others of the architects' projects were combined.

Bienal de Venecia '96

A la invitación de Hans Hollein para intervenir en la Bienal de Venecia bajo el lema: "Sensores del futuro. El arquitecto como sismógrafo", Miralles y Tagliabue respondieron proponiendo un montaje que recogiese las diversas fases y los diferentes proyectos contenidos en el proyecto para el Palacio de los Deportes de Huesca (1988-1994). "Parece" –apuntan los arquitectos– "que el que habla el último tiene razón. Parece que la última construcción es lo único de lo que se puede hablar. Por eso es difícil saltar en el tiempo para actuar como sensores del futuro. Nuestra solución es decir siempre lo mismo, o casi lo mismo. Proponemos pequeñas variantes de un trabajo que no cree que la construcción tenga un sentido de final, de categoría temporal, sino que más bien cree que un proyecto está hecho de instantes inconexos, que dicen cosas

independientes, que se sobreponen... pero que parecen iguales. Tal vez sólo quien es capaz de decir y hacer siempre el mismo movimiento parece avanzar. Esta pequeña vibración puede decir algo sobre el futuro".

La intervención, que recibió el León de Oro, constaba de una maqueta de la primera versión –como ilusión original de ver el edifico completo–, un diorama circular que ilustraba el Palacio en una visión total –interna, externa y cenital– desde el interior de esa suerte anillo mágico, un tríptico al óleo que recogía detalles interiores a escala 1:1, un alfabeto fotográfico de letras formadas por las sombras del edificio, diversas fotos de la ciudad de Huesca y un fotomontaje en blanco y negro en el que se entremezclaban otros proyectos de los arquitectos.

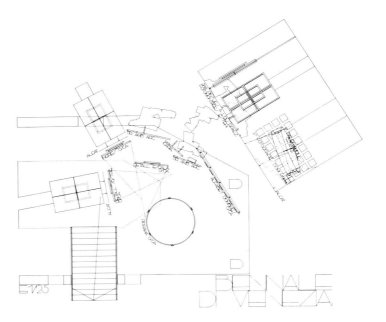

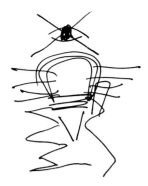

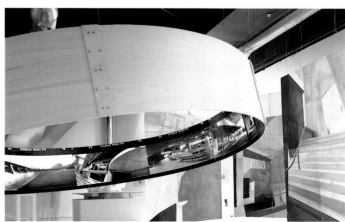

'Shadows and Alphabets'. The Mies van der Rohe Pavilion. Barcelona, 1997

Architects/**Arquitectos:** Enric Miralles & Benedetta Tagliabue
Collaborators/**Colaboradores:** Elena Rocchi,
Fabián Asunción, Germán Zambrana
Installation/**Montaje:** Stéphanie Le Draoullec, Tobias Gottschalk,
Stefan Eckert, Luca Tonella, Nicolai Lund Overgaard,
Ricardo Flores, Lluís Cantallops
Photographs/**Fotografías:** Domi Mora, Giovanni Zanzi

One year later elements similar to those installed in the '96 Venice Biennale occupied a site as historic, and architecturally distinct, as the pavilion designed on Montjuïc by Mies van der Rohe for the Barcelona Universal Exhibition of 1929. The challenge for the architects was to dialog with a given space, one already determined by notions of purity and essentiality. Aside from putting forward a specific layout for the Pavilion, Miralles and Tagliabue supplemented the components of the Venice project with a series of photographs by the anthropologist Domi Mora, creator of a shadow alphabet which already formed part of the exhibition. The snapshots depicted details of the marble veining of the actual pavilion in which figures similar to those in cave painting could be made out. The building was partly distanced from its purism in this way and changed into being a cavern. Purity and abstraction similarly gave way to the festive in the partaking of an outdoor meal.

'Ombres i alfabets'. Pabellón Mies van der Rohe. Barcelona, 1997

Similares elementos a los instalados en la Bienal de Venecia de 1996 ocuparon un año después un lugar histórica y arquitectónicamente tan marcado como el pabellón diseñado en Montjuïc por Mies van der Rohe para la Exposición Universal de Barcelona de 1929. Para los arquitectos, el reto *a priori* era dialogar con un espacio muy determinado por la pureza y la esencialidad.
Amén de plantear una distribución específica para el pabellón, Miralles y Tagliabue añadieron a los componentes del proyecto veneciano una serie de fotografías del antropólogo Domi Mora, autor del alfabeto de sombras que ya formaba parte de la exposición. Las instantáneas recogían detalles de vetas del mármol del propio pabellón, en las que se podían intuir figuras similares a las de las pinturas rupestres. De esta manera, el edificio se alejaba, en cierto modo, de su purismo para convertirse en cueva. Así mismo, la pureza y la abstracción dieron paso a lo festivo mediante la celebración de una comida en el exterior.

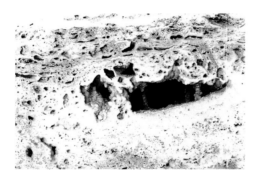

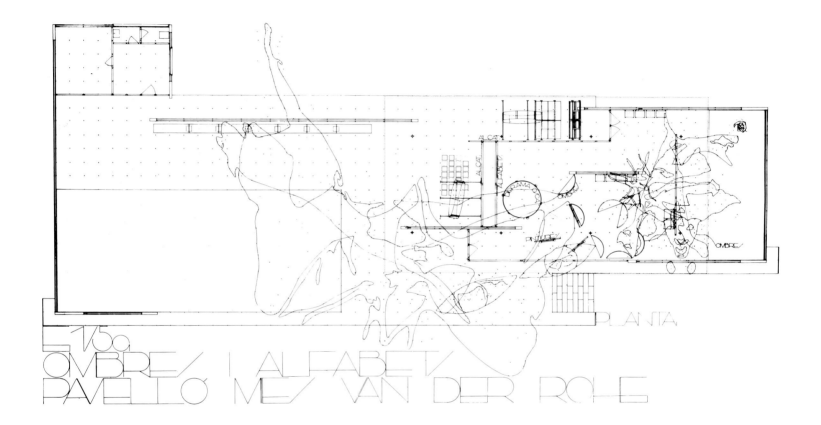

The Nordic Tour. 1998

Architects/**Arquitectos:** Enric Miralles & Benedetta Tagliabue
AAA Vibeke Linde Strandby & Mogens Brandt Poulsen
Collaborator/**Colaborador:** Anne Galmar
EMBT: Elena Rocchi, Fabián Asunción
Collaborators/**Colaboradores:** Carlos Alberto Ruiz, Ana María Romero

Successive exhibitions in Stockholm (Sweden), Copenhagen and Århus (Denmark) grew out of the notion of the journey. Linked to this notion was the architects' exploration of the actual nature of the pieces exhibited. Given that their nature was, in short, that they had to travel, Miralles and Tagliabue decided to leave them in the boxes they were being transported in. In this way the boxes framing the exhibits occupied the gallery space and created an order which was changed on each new leg of the journey. "I don't like things hanging on the walls," Miralled argues. "On the floor each object is integrated into the landscape, in the same way that a building uses the ground as a material for working with." Just as in Marcel Duchamp's 'Boîte-en-valise', the Nordic Tour, unlike other exhibitions, forms a complete portable display of the architectures of the Miralles-Tagliabue studio. Projects like the pergolas of the Olympic Village, the Igualada Cemetery, the Archery Range for Barcelona '92, the house for Kolonihaven, or the National Archive, Auditorium and Royal Theater in Copenhagen were present as drawings, models and photomontages that were complemented by the photographic alphabet, the ring-shaped diorama of Huesca and a tunnel built with sectional drawings. Aside from the outer journey, the Tour proposed an inner one in which the spectator was invited to contemplate the works as an experience of continuity that proceeded from the specificity of one place to that of another, from one project to the next.

El *tour* nórdico. 1998

La sucesivas exposiciones en Estocolmo (Suecia), Copenhague y Århus (Dinamarca) nacieron bajo el espíritu del viaje. A este espíritu se unía la investigación de los arquitectos en torno a la realidad de las piezas expuestas. Dado que su realidad era, sencillamente, que tenían que viajar, Miralles y Tagliabue decidieron dejarlas en las cajas en que eran transportadas. De este modo, las cajas como base de las piezas ocupaban el espacio de la sala y creaban un orden que cambiaba en cada nueva estación del viaje. "No me gustan– sostiene Miralles– las cosas colgando de las paredes. En el suelo cada obra se integra en el paisaje, igual que un edificio usa el suelo como material con el que trabajar".

A la manera de la *Boîte-en-valise* de Marcel Duchamp, *El tour nórdico* constituye, como ninguna otra exposición, una completa muestra portátil de las arquitecturas del estudio Miralles-Tagliabue. Proyectos como la pérgolas de la Villa Olímpica, el Cementerio de Igualada, el Tiro con Arco para Barcelona '92, la casa para Kolonihaven o el Archivo Nacional, el Auditorio y el Teatro Real de Copenhague estaban presentes en dibujos, maquetas y fotomontajes que se completaban con el alfabeto fotográfico y el diorama anular de Huesca, y con un túnel construido con dibujos de secciones. Además del viaje exterior, el *Tour* planteaba uno interior en que el espectador era invitado a contemplar las obras como una experiencia de continuidad que iba desde la especificidad de un lugar a la de otro, desde un proyecto al siguiente.

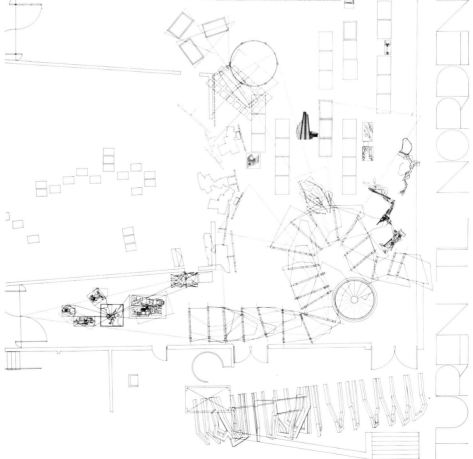

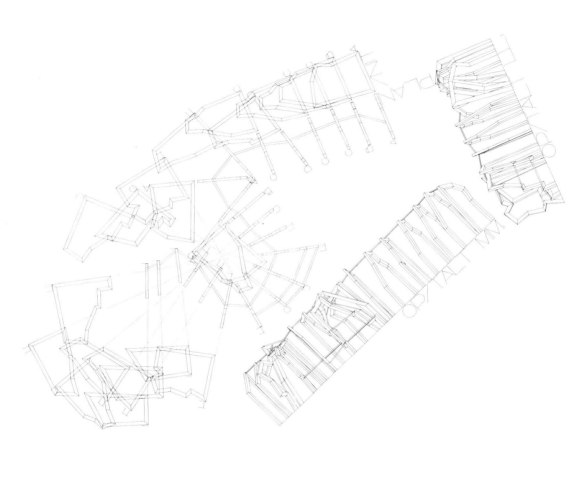

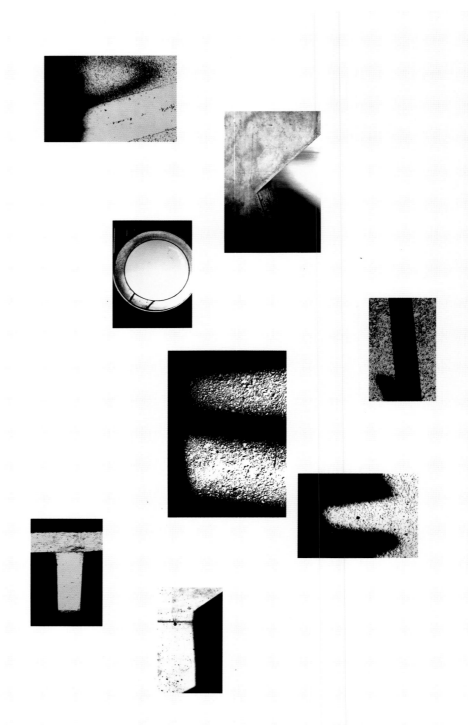

Enric Miralles & Benedetta Tagliabue
Arquitectes Associats

The Nordic Tour
1997-1998

Århus
Arkitektskolen i Aarhus
november

Stockholm
Konstakademien
januar-februar

København
Kunstakademiets Arkitektskole
april

Credits: AAA Vibeke Linde Strandby & Mogens Brandt Poulsen   Elena Rocchi & Fabian Asunción   Stockholm Cultural Capital '98

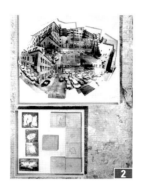
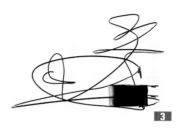

1-2 **Desterrat.** Pi i Sunyer Monument. Barcelona, 1995.
3-4 **Ocells.** The Inhabited Garden. El jardín habitado. Barnaola Gallery. Barcelona, 1992.
5-6 **Instalation in l'Uniteé.** Firminy, 1993.
7 **AEDES.** Berlin, 1993.
8 **Architektur Forum.** Zurich.
9-10 **Le Situationie.** MACBA, Barcelona, 1996.
11-12 **Architektur Centrum.** Wien, 1993.

Exhibition in the Graduate School of Design. Harvard. 1993

Architect/**Arquitecto:** Enric Miralles
Installation/**Montaje:** Enric Miralles,
Benedetta Tagliabue, Brooke Hodge, Piper Rankine,
and the 'Lectures and Exhibitions' staff of G.S.D.

For the mounting of the monographic exhibition of his work, organized in Harvard during his residency as Kenzo Tange Professor, Enric Miralles proposed a series of projects that were combined with each other. In this way the juxtaposition of designs for the Readers' Circle in Madrid, the Huesca Sports Palace and the Igualada Cemetery ended up forming a continuous floorplan installed as a 21-meter-long mural on one of the walls of the Gund Hall Gallery. Together with this the architect mounted various photo collages of different buildings on half-cylinders of glass. This device aimed at endowing the display with a structure that not only illustrated the projects, but also created a new reality for the public who visited the school. Finally, Miralles hoped that the exhibition of the floorplans of various works - with all their geometrical precision - might communicate to the different places in which they were exhibited something of the spirit of the original surroundings for which they had been planned. "Different moments in the life of a number of projects were exhibited," the architect concludes. "Maybe this is a confusing way of recording the works, but it's the same confusion that exists when each of them is conceived".

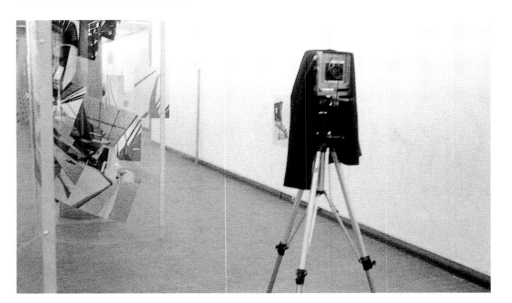

Exposición en la Graduate School of Design, Harvard, 1993

Para el montaje de la exposición monográfica sobre su obra, celebrada en Harvard durante su estancia como profesor en la cátedra Kenzo Tange, Enric Miralles dispuso una serie de proyectos que se mezclaban entre sí. De este modo, la yuxtaposición de dibujos del Círculo de Lectores de Madrid, el Palacio de los Deportes de Huesca o el Cementerio de Igualada terminó formando una planta montada a modo de mural a lo largo de los 21 metros de una de las paredes de la Gund Hall Gallery.

Por otro lado, el arquitecto dispuso varios *collages* fotográficos de diferentes construcciones sobre semicilindros de vidrio. Este recurso pretendía que la representación adquiriese un cuerpo que no sólo ilustrase los proyectos, sino que constituyese también una nueva realidad para el público que visitaba la Escuela. Finalmente, Miralles intentó que la exposición de las plantas de diversos trabajos –con toda su precisión geométrica– llevase a los diferentes lugares en los que se exhibía parte del espíritu del entorno original para el que habían sido proyectados. "Se exhibían –concluye el arquitecto– diferentes momentos en la vida de algunos proyectos. Es tal vez una forma confusa de recordar las obras, pero es la misma confusión que existe cuando se concibe cada una de ellas".

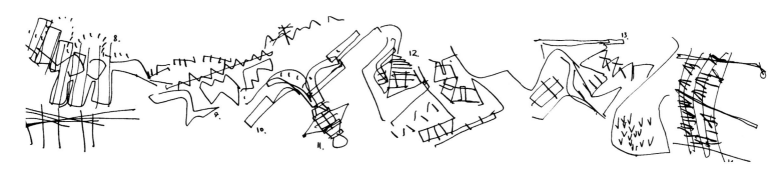

Prospa Stand
Paris. 1997
The German Pavilion ARCO '96
Madrid. 1996

Fair to fair

While using their particular language, the stands Enric Miralles and Benedetta Tagliabue have done for various fairs adapt to a given, enclosed space and to predetermined commercial aims. Of necessity the temporal nature of these projects conjoins speed of assembly with lightness and functionality. Added to this is the undeniably representational character of such works, for which the architecture has to be self-evident without, for all that, ceasing to be enigmatic; that's to say, it has to display things while also displaying itself. Concepts like solidity, lightness, transparency, versatility and in certain cases adaptability enter into play in nomadic works that are meant to be something sedentary for a few days. The architects themselves are transformed into travellers –travelling salesmen, if you like– who put up their structures for a limited amount of time. As in the exhibitions devoted to their own oeuvre, in these works Miralles and Tagliabue are once again acting, Isozaki would say, as *marevitos*, strolling players who go from place to place displaying their wares and, in passing, broadcasting the latest news. Required to build things in the micro-world of merchandising –be it artistic as in Madrid, or pharmaceutical as in Paris– the architects know that, like the salesmen, they too work in the space of the temporal, in the ephemeral and perpetual present, at the mid-point between remembering and forgetting.

De feria en **feria**

Los *stands* para ferias de Enric Miralles y Benedetta Tagliabue se adaptan, desde un lenguaje propio, a un espacio dado dentro de un recinto y a una finalidad comercial establecida de antemano. La temporalidad de estos proyectos conjuga necesariamente la rapidez de montaje con la ligereza y la funcionalidad. A todo ello hay que añadir el carácter ineludiblemente representativo de estos trabajos, por lo que la arquitectura ha de ser clara sin dejar de ser enigmática, es decir, ha de mostrar sin dejar de mostrarse. Conceptos como solidez, levedad, transparencia, versatilidad y, en algunos casos, adaptabilidad entran en juego en obras nómadas destinadas a transformarse en sedentarias por unos días. Los propios arquitectos se transforman en viajeros –viajantes, si se quiere– que levantan sus estructuras por un tiempo limitado.

Como en las exposiciones dedicadas a su propia obra, en estos trabajos, Miralles y Tagliabue vuelven a actuar, diría Isozaki, como *marevitos* que van de lugar en lugar mostrando su labor y transmitiendo, de paso, las noticias. Llamados a construir en el microcosmos de la mercancía –ya sea artística como en Madrid o farmacéutica como en París– los arquitectos saben que, como los feriantes, también ellos trabajan en el espacio de lo temporal, en el presente efímero y perpetuo, a medio camino entre la memoria y el olvido.

Prospa Stand. Paris 1997

Architects/**Arquitectos:** Enric Miralles & Benedetta Tagliabue
Collaborators/**Colaboradores:** Anne Galmar,
Piercarlo Comacchio, Julie Nicaise
Installation/**Montaje:** Caledoscopi
Client/**Cliente:** Prospa, Valerio Ferrari

One fundamental idea guided Enric Miralles and Benedetta Tagliabue when addressing a project first constructed in the Paris Conference Center in 1997 and still doing the rounds today: since the products could not be directly displayed, the stand was to have a high-tech feel that would symbolize the Prospa Company's own pharmaceutical technology. And all this without renouncing the kind of inviting image that would cause the public to stop and look. Added to which it was essential that the stand be easily dismounted, transported and adapted to different trade fair contexts.
The architects accordingly designed a 24 m2 space occupied by a series of metal tripods with mobile screens made up of wooden frames, plus a lightweight titanium mesh on which the Prospa logo was printed. This element combines advertising and a host of transparent and reflecting surfaces which allude to the importance of water for the pharmaceutical industry. Since the issue is more one of information than of display, the layout of the screens permits open exhibition and semi-private meeting areas to be created without losing visual contact between inside and outside. Finally, adaptability and transport are facilitated by integrating the packing cases into the construction and by using a modular flooring of wood. Seen in plan, each module would correspond to a letter of the alphabet.

Prospa Stand. Paris 1997

Una idea fundamental guió a Enric Miralles y Benedetta Tagliabue a la hora de enfrentarse a un proyecto que se construyó por primera vez en el Palacio de Congresos de París en 1997 y que en la actualidad sigue viajando: ya que los productos no podían exponerse directamente, el *stand* debía tener un aspecto de alta tecnología que representara la tecnología farmacéutica de la empresa Prospa. Todo ello sin renunciar a una imagen confortable que invitase al público a pararse. Por otro lado, era fundamental que el *stand* pudiese ser fácilmente desmontado, transportado y adaptado a los diferentes espacios feriales. Con estas premisas, los arquitectos proyectaron un espacio de 24 m² ocupado por una serie de trípodes metálicos con mamparas móviles formadas por marcos de madera con una malla ligera de titanio en la que se serigrafió el logotipo de Prospa. Este elemento conjuga la publicidad con un juego de transparencias y reflejos que remite a la importancia del agua en la industria farmacéutica. Dado que se trata más de informar que de exponer, la distribución de las mamparas permite crear zonas abiertas de exposición y zonas semiprivadas de reunión sin perder el contacto visual entre interior y exterior. Finalmente, la adaptabilidad y el transporte se facilitan integrando en la construcción las cajas de embalaje y usando un pavimento modular de madera. A cada módulo correspondería, visto en planta, una de las letras del alfabeto.

The German Pavilion. ARCO '96 Art Fair. Madrid

Architect/**Arquitecto:** Enric Miralles
Collaborators/**Colaboradores:** Elena Rocchi,
Hans Christian Pedersen, Aria Djalali, Marion Guinard

In this pavilion design for the Madrid Contemporary Art Fair Enric Miralles planned a see-through labyrinth of movable forms, suitable for handling the widely diverging material on display. His intention was to create spaces that were different but equal in importance, and in which the visitor might linger during his visit. A wood specialist made the pine structure for the different thematic areas of the exhibition: videos, photos, models, multiples, books... The architect proposed an ongoing tour with different areas for each particular section. The documentary material was displayed on horizontal surfaces, therefore, leaving the vertical plane for blocks of information material. Given that transparency was one of the key proposals of this work, the documents could be looked at from both sides of the dividing walls. The spectator was thereby integrated into an architectural ambiance which underlined the fragility of the physical structure while emphasizing its conceptual nature.

As the Deutsche Bank collection was to be added to the 'Germany in Arco 96' display, Miralles' scheme was transformed into something more closed for this collection. For that reason he attempted to augment the protection of the drawings on display by creating a separate, highly discreet entrance in the framework of the main structure; at the same time he used a finer wood for this. Transparency was sacrificed for solidity in the panelwork and the circulations were changed into rooms.

Pabellón de Alemania. Feria de arte ARCO '96. Madrid

En este proyecto de pabellón para la Feria de Arte Contemporáneo de Madrid, Enric Miralles planteó un laberinto transparente de perfiles mutables para enfrentarse a la disparidad del contenido a exhibir. Su intención era crear espacios, diferentes pero de idéntica importancia, en los que el visitante pudiera detenerse durante su visita. Un único expositor de madera de pino formaba el perfil espacial de las diferentes áreas temáticas de la exposición –vídeos, fotos, maquetas, múltiples, libros...–.
El arquitecto proponía un recorrido continuo con diferentes zonas para cada ámbito específico.
Así, el material documental se expondría sobre superficies horizontales, dejando el plano vertical para disponer los bloques informativos. Dado que la transparencia era una de las propuestas centrales de este trabajo, los documentos podrían ser mirados desde ambos lados de las paredes divisorias. De este modo se integra al espectador en un ambiente arquitectónico en el que se subraya la fragilidad de la estructura física para resaltar su carácter conceptual.
Puesto que a la muestra "Alemania en Arco '96" se añadía la colección del Deutsche Bank, la propuesta de Miralles se tornaba, para dicha colección, más cerrada. Así trataba de facilitar la protección de los dibujos expuestos: creaba un acceso independiente, discretamente abierto entre los bastidores de la estructura central; al mismo tiempo, utilizaba una madera más noble.
De este modo, la transparencia pasaba a ser solidez en los paneles macizos y los recorridos se transformaban en habitaciones.

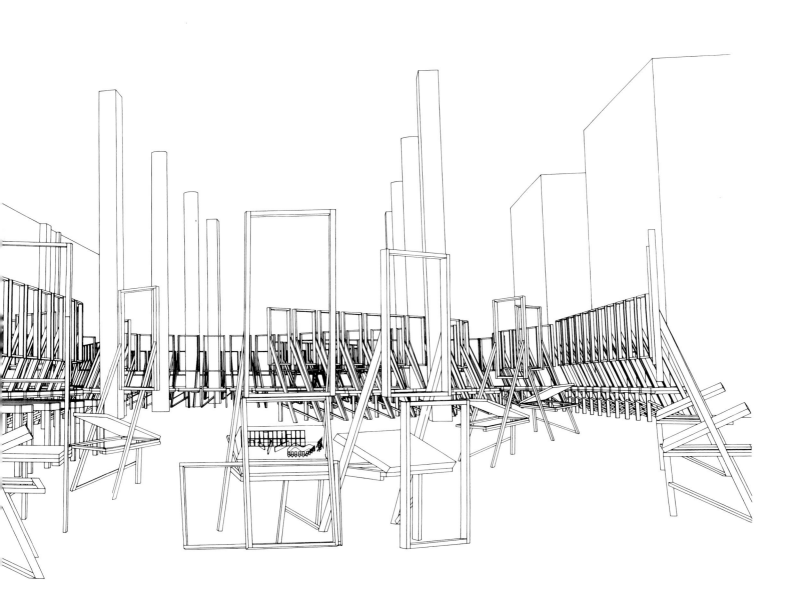

Alphabet
Huesca. Spain. 1994
"Mai per atzar" Opera
Miralles Tagliabue Studio. Barcelona. 1996
Pergolas
Olympic Village. Barcelona. 1992
Lelukaappi
Jyväskylä. Finland. 1995

Intermezzo

"We've never considered," Enric Miralles and Benedetta Tagliabue claim, "that the constructional process ought to concentrate on the objective of vision alone. Doing away with vision's main role is useful for recognizing the differing logics there are in a project."

The shadow a building projects is also architecture. It could be argued that without light there is no form and without shadow there is no light. "Light is basically the visible animal of the invisible," the Cuban writer José Lezama Lima once said. The alphabet formed accidentally by the shadows of the Huesca Sports Palace have an aleatory and festive quality that comes together in the set designs of an opera called - and this is no accident –'Never By Chance'–, as if the time and space of each project were speaking an untraduceable language: just as no two theatrical performances are ever quite the same, so the shadow of a building inevitably depends on the place and the time of year. And the playfulness of a number of pergolas, street theater meant to become shadow-play, is likewise encountered in a toy filling the child's space like some ur-theater in which each play session is a singular event. Like a zigzagging detour made along the way, these intermezzos propose new and wider-ranging ways of looking at the work of Miralles and Tagliabue, a work in which the final result is more than the sum of the parts.

Intermezzo

"Nunca hemos creído" –afirman Enric Miralles y Benedetta Tagliabue– "que el proceso constructivo se centrase en el único objetivo de la visión. Eliminar el papel principal de la visión es útil para reconocer las distintas lógicas que hay dentro de un proyecto".

La sombra que proyecta un edificio también es arquitectura. Podría decirse que sin luz no hay forma y sin sombra no hay luz. "La luz es el primer animal visible de lo invisible", escribió el escritor cubano José Lezama Lima. El abecedario que formaron caprichosamente las sombras del Palacio de los Deportes de Huesca participa de lo azaroso que se une a lo festivo en la escenografía de una ópera –no por casualidad llamada, precisamente, *Nunca por azar*–, como si el tiempo y los espacios de cada proyecto hablasen un idioma intransferible: igual que una representación teatral nunca se repite idéntica, la sombra de una construcción depende ineludiblemente de la estación y el lugar. Del mismo modo, lo lúdico de unas pérgolas, que quieren ser un dinámico pasacalles destinado a convertirse en sombra, se encuentra en un juguete que ocupa el espacio infantil a modo de primer teatro del mundo, en el que cada sesión de juego es también irrepetible. Como movimientos en zigzag dentro de un viaje, estos intermedios plantean nuevos puntos de vista y completan una visión global de la obra de Miralles y Tagliabue en la que el resultado total es algo más que la simple suma de las partes.

Huesca Alphabet. 1994

The photos by the anthropologist Domi Mora that make up this alphabet are of the fleeting shadows created in various parts of the Huesca Sports Palace, built between 1988 and 1994. The alphabet project grows out of Miralles and Tagliabue's interest in shifting the customary viewpoint when photographing architecture. To do this the Palace is variously contemplated from between the trees, pillars and fences, or from a worm's-eye view. In other photos, the alphabet ones in particular, attention is paid to both the abstraction of the light and shade and to the figuration of the letters. The architects, then, seek to portray not just a building but its effects; in short, to present a more complex idea of it. When photography goes beyond the traditional limits of vision it thereby forms part of this complexity.

Architect/**Arquitecto:** Enric Miralles
Photographs/**Fotografías:** Domi Mora

Alfabeto Huesca. 1994

La serie de fotografías del antropólogo Domi Mora que constituye este alfabeto se tomaron al capricho de las sombras formadas en distintos puntos del Palacio de los Deportes de Huesca, construido entre 1988 y 1994. El proyecto de abecedario surge del interés de Miralles y Tagliabue por desplazar el punto de vista ordinario a la hora de fotografiar la arquitectura. Para conseguirlo, en algunas instantáneas se contempla el Palacio desde el bosque de árboles, pilares y tablas, o a ras de tierra, **casi como una hormiga . En otras, las del alfabeto concretamente, se atiende a la abstracción de la luz y la sombra y, al mismo tiempo, a la figuración de las letras. De este modo, los arquitectos pretenden retratar no sólo un edificio, sino también sus efectos y a la vez plantear un pensamiento complejo. Cuando la fotografía sobrepasa los límites tradicionales de la visión pasa a formar parte de dicha complejidad.**

'Mai per atzar'/'Never By Chance'. Barcelona. 1997

The one-act opera 'Never By Chance' was presented on 11 April 1997 on the occasion of the inauguration of the new Enric Miralles and Benedetta Tagliabue studio on the Passatje de la Pau in Barcelona's old town. The idea, libretto and direction are by Valerio Ferrari. The music is the work of Roberto Cacciapaglia. As the performance unfolded the drawings being executing at that precise moment by the architects were projected from their worktables onto both stage and actors. The set design was completed by pieces of furniture hanging down above the stage and by the schematic representation of a wickerwork rock —essential to the narrative— with echoes of the Tateyama project. The feeling of travelling through time produced during the show, plus the show's *opera prima* status, were made manifest when the building intended for a studio, in their début work, changes to become a theater.

Libretto/**Libreto:** Valerio Ferrari
Music and piano/**Música y piano:** Roberto Cacciapaglia
Electric guitar/**Guitarra eléctrica:** Andrea Rossi
Epicasta/Winnie: Uma Isamat
Agamedes/Willie: Andreu Carandell
Hermes: Julio Manrique
Drawings/**Dibujos:** Enric Miralles, Benedetta Tagliabue,
Eva Prats, Ricardo Flores
Sets, costume design and props/**Escenografía, vestuario y *atrezzo*:**
Estudio Miralles-Tagliabue
Set-building/**Construcción:** Fabià Asunción, Stefan Eckert, Luca Tonella
Costumes/**Vestuario:** Valeria Civil

'Mai per atzar','Nunca por azar'. Barcelona, 1997

La ópera en un acto *Mai per atzar –Nunca por azar–* se puso en escena el 11 del abril de 1997 con motivo de la inauguración del nuevo estudio de Enric Miralles y Benedetta Tagliabue en el Passatge de la Pau, en el casco antiguo de Barcelona. La idea, el libreto y la dirección son de Valerio Ferrari. La música es obra de Roberto Cacciapaglia. A medida que avanzaba la representación se proyectaban sobre el escenario y los actores los dibujos que los arquitectos ejecutaban en ese preciso instante desde sus mesas. La escenografía se completaba con algunos muebles que se descolgaban sobre la escena y con la representación esquemática en tiras de mimbre de una roca –fundamental en el argumento– con ecos del proyecto de Tateyama.

El viaje en el tiempo que se produce en la representación y el carácter de ópera prima estaban muy presente cuando el edificio destinado a ser estudio, en su obra primera, se convierte en teatro.

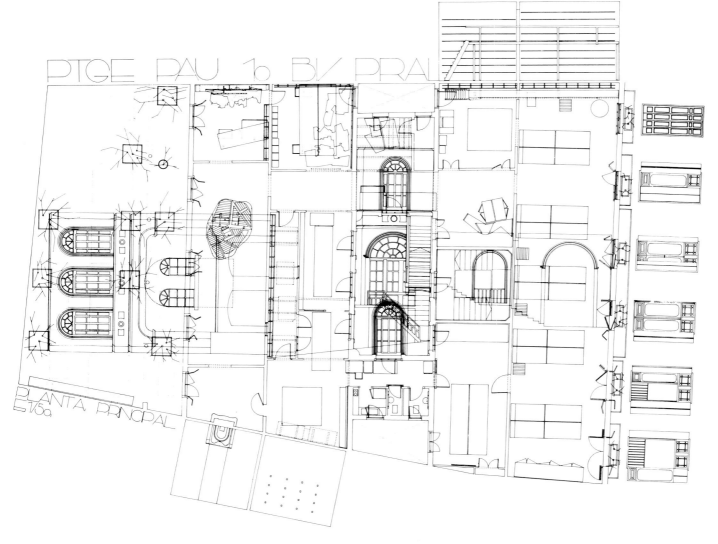

'Mai per atzar'/'Never By Chance'. The Play.

Agamedes, architect of the temple of Delphi, receives a visit from Hermes, who brings him a commission from Zeus to construct a rock in which to guard all his gold. Agamedes is mistrustful, alleging that he never manages to get paid for his work.
Epicasta, the wife of Agamedes, is a very passionate woman. She is worried because, aside from being penniless, a camel has fallen sick. On receiving Zeus' commission Epicasta, too, is mistrustful, although she will end up urging her husband to construct the rock and even collaborate in its construction.
Hermes, Zeus' messenger, has to convince Agamedes to accept the commission. The task is a difficult one, but his long friendship with the architect will help matters. On top of that Hermes will be the one entrusted with making 2,700 years of history flash by and of setting us down in the 20th century before two other characters, Willie and Winnie, the heroes of Samuel Beckett's *Happy Days*.
Willie and Winnie, the modern versions of the architect and his wife, are, in 'Never By Chance', two American tourists lost in the Pyrenees after having walked upwards of 30,000 paces. It is they who will find by chance, twenty-seven centuries later, the rock constructed by Agamedes and Epicasta, and have free access to Zeus' gold.

'Mai per atzar'. 'Nunca por azar'. La Ópera.

Agamedes, el arquitecto del templo de Delfos, recibe la visita de Hermes, que le lleva de parte de Zeus el encargo de construir una roca en la que guardar todo su oro. Agamedes desconfía, alegando que nunca consigue cobrar los honorarios por sus trabajos.
Epicasta, la mujer de Agamedes, es una mujer inclinada a las pasiones. Está preocupada porque, además de no tener ni un céntimo, un camello ha enfermado. Al recibir el encargo de Zeus también Epicasta desconfía, aunque terminará animando a su marido a construir la roca y colaborando activamente en su construcción. Hermes, el enviado de Zeus, tiene que convencer a Agamedes de que acepte el encargo.

La tarea es difícil pero su vieja amistad con el arquitecto facilitará las cosas. Hermes será además el encargado de dejar pasar dos mil setecientos años de historia y de situarnos en el siglo XX, delante de dos protagonistas más: Willie y Winnie, los héroes de la obra de Samuel Beckett *Días felices*.
Willie y Winnie, las transfiguraciones modernas del arquitecto y su mujer, son en *Mai per atzar* dos turistas americanos perdidos en los Pirineos después de caminar más de 30.000 pasos. Serán ellos los que, por azar, encontrarán, veintisiete siglos más tarde, la roca construida por Agamedes y Epicasta y, por lo tanto, tendrán libre acceso al oro de Zeus.

Pergolas in the Olympic Village. Avenida Icaria. Barcelona. 1992

In his pergolas for this recently constructed avenue Enric Miralles tried to evoke the festive atmosphere of street theater and also to open up and close off the pathway to pedestrians using a rhythm different to that of other streets in the Olympic Village: "Gradually," says the architect, "the avenue ceases being an avenue and instead becomes a series of houses around little patios." The project is made up of a succession of cantilevered posts that support a secondary structure which in turn supports the wooden elements completing the whole. The rhythm of these elements attempts to create, along the walkway, an undulating horizon line for linking the buildings in the area to the distant profile of the Montjuïc mountain.

Architect/**Arquitecto:** Enric Miralles
Preplanning/**Anteproyecto:** Enric Miralles & Carme Pinós
Structures/**Estructuras:** B.O.M.A.
Contractor/**Constructor:** Delgado
Builders/**Aparejadores:** EDETCO
Collaborators/**Colaboradores:** J.Callis, G.M. Godoy, F. Pla

Pérgolas en la Villa Olímpica de Barcelona. Avenida Icaria. Barcelona, 1992

En sus pérgolas para esta larga avenida de nueva construcción, Enric Miralles trató de evocar el ambiente festivo de un pasacalles a la vez que intentó abrir y cerrar el camino a los paseantes con un ritmo diferente del resto de las calles de la Villa Olímpica: "A su paso –dice el arquitecto–, la avenida deja de serlo para ser una sucesión de viviendas alrededor de unos patios de vecinos".

El proyecto está formado por una sucesión de mástiles en voladizo que sostienen una estructura secundaria en la que, a su vez, se apoyan las piezas de madera que culminan el conjunto. El ritmo de las piezas trata de crear, en el interior del paseo, una línea de paisaje que conecte las distintas edificaciones con el perfil lejano de la montaña de Montjuïc.

'Lelukaappi'. 1995

Architect/**Arquitecto:** Enric Miralles
Collaborators/**Colaboradores:** Teiji Autio, Ricardo Flores,
Thomas Mival, Torsten Massek, Phillip Dietrich

Subsequent to a commission from the Alvar Aalto Museum in Jyväskylä (Finland) to create a prototype piece of furniture that might bear on Finnish architecture, Enric Miralles invented a sort of children's theater on wheels intended for the play area of the Mollet del Vallés 'Ludoteca'.

Given its mobile nature Lelukaappi can be related to the architect's other furniture, such as the 'UnsTable', since like that piece it can be filled up with objects, and may be opened and closed. Miralles himself, meanwhile, relates this prototype to 'Heaven', his Tateyama installation, given that in the latter light occupies space in the same way the 1.80-meter-high toy occupies the children's room, as well as being lived in by them. And just as the Japanese project created a cloud by means of different sections, so this piece of furniture takes its shape from various planes of wood that open and close.

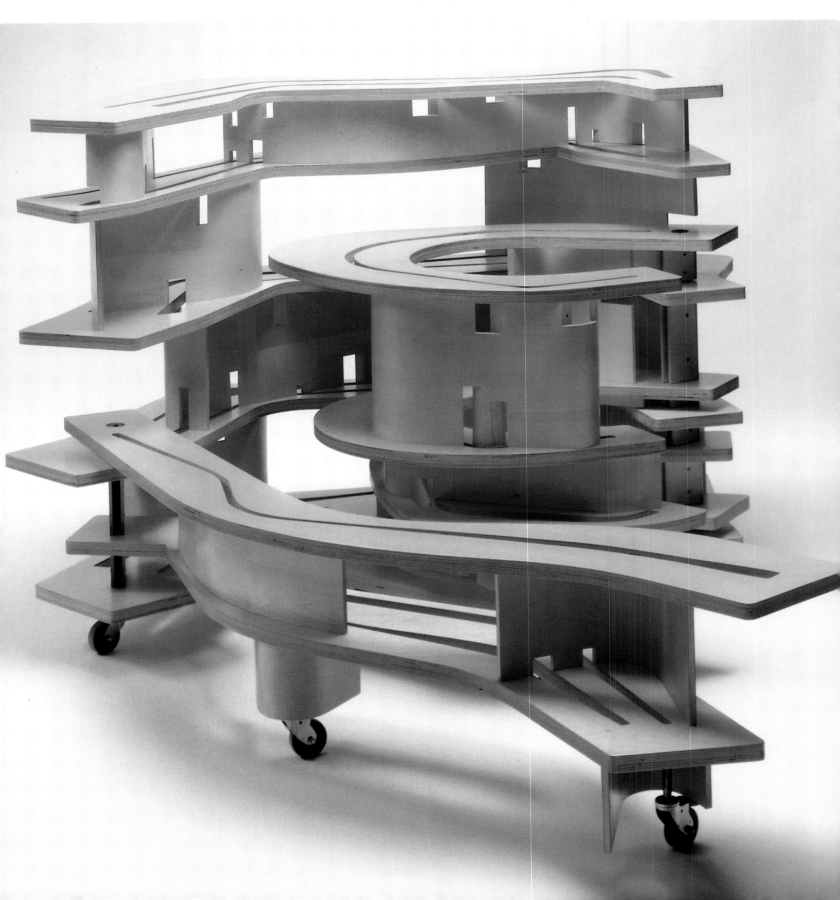

'Lelukaappi'. 1995

A partir de un encargo del museo Alvar Aalto de Jyväskylä (Finlandia) para realizar un prototipo de mueble que pudiera relacionarse con la arquitectura finlandesa, Enric Miralles desarrolló una suerte de teatro infantil con ruedas destinado a la zona de juegos de la ludoteca de Mollet del Vallés.

Por su movilidad, Lelukaappi podría emparentarse con otros muebles del arquitecto, como la mesa InesTable, ya que, como aquélla, puede llenarse de objetos, abrirse y cerrarse. Además, el propio Miralles relaciona este prototipo con Heaven, la instalación de Tateyama, ya que en ésta la luz ocupa el espacio, como el juguete, de aproximadamente 1,80 m de alto, ocupa la habitación de los niños al tiempo que puede ser habitado por ellos. Por otro lado, igual que el proyecto japonés creaba una nube por medio de secciones, el mueble toma forma mediante planos de madera que se abren y se cierran

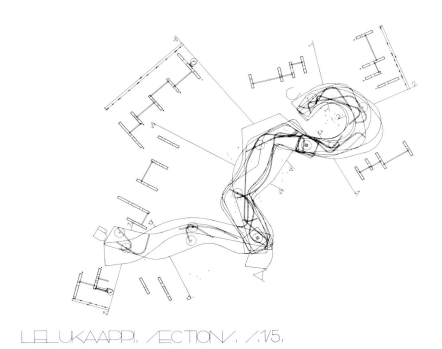

LELUKAAPPI. SECTIONS. /:1/5.

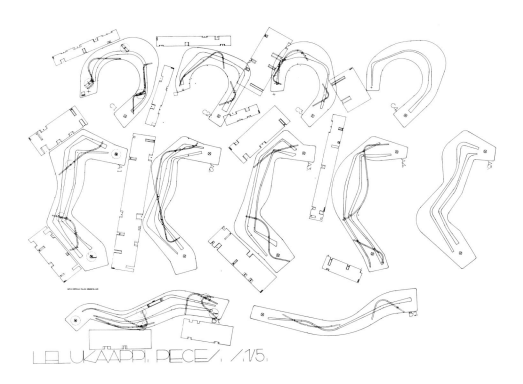

LELUKAAPPI. PECES. /:1/5.

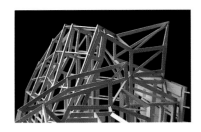

De l'espai no t'en refiïs mai (II)
Barnola Gallery. Barcelona. 1997
Wooden House
Kolonihaven. Copenhagen. 1996
Domus Totem
Milan. 1998
Abitare La Masieri
Palazzeto Masieri. Venice. 1997
Paseos
Spanish Academy. Rome. 1995
Heaven
Tateyama Museum-Park. Japan. 1995

Six **installations**

"Nobody is merely a sculptor, a painter or an architect," says Le Corbusier. "All artistic creation is on the way to becoming poetry." There is, in principle, no visual manifestation as near to architecture as the installation. Both are conceived for a defined space, with the rider that, unlike architecture, the time span of the installation is, in principle, also defined beforehand. And in no other century but the twentieth has it been this way. The moment sculpture comes down from its pedestal and takes a path that extends beyond the old-fashioned idea of the monument, the architectonic appears, emphatically and without limits, both in public art of an urban kind and in Land Art, minimalism and installation art.

Cognizant of the sheer diversity of locations, Enric Miralles and Benedetta Tagliabue have installed site-specific works in a museum-park pavilion, in a cloister next to Bramante's temple, in a Venetian palace and in an art gallery. Next to integration in the city and a preoccupation with time, as in Milan, experimenting with light and immateriality in Japan, or the importance of tradition and *genius loci* in Rome, habitability determined their projects in Venice, Copenhagen and Barcelona.

Seis **instalaciones**

"Nadie es sólo escultor, sólo pintor o sólo arquitecto" –dice Le Corbusier–. "Toda creación artística está encaminada a la poesía".

Ninguna manifestación plástica hay, en principio, tan cercana a la arquitectura como la instalación. Ambas se conciben para un espacio definido, con el matiz de que, a diferencia de la arquitectura, el tiempo de la instalación también está, en principio, definido de antemano. Y en ningún otro siglo ha sido esto así como en el xx. Desde que la escultura se baja del pedestal y toma caminos que van más allá de la idea decimonónica de monumento, lo arquitectónico aparece, sin límites y de manera decisiva, tanto en el arte público de carácter urbano, como en el *land-art*, el minimal o las instalaciones.

Atendiendo a una gran diversidad de emplazamientos, Enric Miralles y Benedetta Tagliabue colocaron obras específicas en un pabellón de un parque-museo, en un claustro contiguo al templete de Bramante, en un palacio veneciano o en una galería de arte.

Junto a la integración en una ciudad y la preocupación por el tiempo, como en Milán, la experimentación con la luz y lo inmaterial, en Japón, o la importancia de la tradición y del *genius loci*, en Roma, la habitabilidad determinó sus proyectos en Venecia, Copenhague y Barcelona.

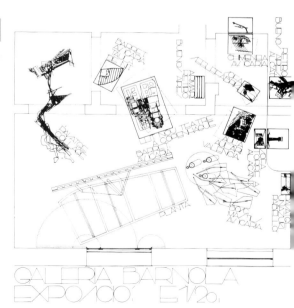

'De l'espai no t'en refiïs mai (II)'/'Never Trust in Space (II)'. Antonio de Barnola Gallery. Barcelona. 1997

Architects/**Arquitectos:** Enric Miralles & Benedetta Tagliabue
Collaborators/**Colaboradores:** Calderería Delgado, Fabián Asunción,
Stefan Eckert, George Mahnke, Tobi Aus der Beek

In their installation for the Antonio de Barnola Gallery, 'Never Trust in Space (II)', Enric Miralles and Benedetta Tagliabue tried to create a living area in which concepts like space, size, location, construction, objectivity, subjectivity, reality and memory would be intertwined, questioned and redefined. A prototype pergola designed to be positioned horizontally in the open space of the Avenida Icaria radically changed size, it would seem, when installed the right way up in the confined space of the gallery. Just as the prototype —which rather than being a presence on the street became an indoor presence instead— functioned as a kind of doorway to the room, so other fragments and maquettes from various projects managed to evoke different elements of a house in terms of its form and dimensions: roof (Icaria rooftops), landscape (Archery Range, Alicante Sports Palace and the Meditation Block in Unazuki, Japan, among others), bedside table (Icaria ceiling), bed (Copenhagen Royal Theater), wardrobe (Retiro Park, Buenos Aires), chimney (model of the Icaria rooftops), armchair (Seele Glass factory, Germany), table (Valencia classroom block), easy chair (Alicante Airport control tower) and garden (structure of the Icaria roof pillars).

"De l'espai no te'n refiïs mai (II)". Galería Antonio de Barnola. Barcelona, 1997

En su instalación *Del espacio nunca te fíes (II)* para la Galería Antonio de Barnola, Enric Miralles y Benedetta Tagliabue trataron de crear una habitación en la que se mezclaran, cuestionaran y redefinieran conceptos como los de espacio, dimensión, situación, construcción, objetividad, subjetividad, realidad y memoria. Así, un prototipo de pérgola, destinado a ser colocado horizontalmente en el espacio abierto de la avenida Icaria, hacía cambiar radicalmente la impresión de su tamaño al ser instalado de pie en el espacio cerrado de la galería. Del mismo modo que el prototipo –que dejaba de ser una pieza de ciudad para serlo de interior– funcionaba a modo de puerta para la habitación, otros elementos y maquetas de diferentes proyectos pasaban a evocar diversos elementos de una vivienda en función de su forma y dimensiones: techo (cubiertas de Icaria), paisaje (Tiro con Arco, Palacio de los Deportes de Alicante y Pabellón de Meditación de Unazuki, Japón, entre otros), mesilla de noche (techo de las cubiertas de Icaria), cama (Teatro Real de Copenhague), armario (parque del área del Retiro, Buenos Aires), chimenea (maqueta de las cubiertas de Icaria), sillón (fábrica de vidrio Seele, Alemania), mesa (aulario de Valencia), butaca (torre de control del aeropuerto de Alicante) y jardín (estructura de los pilares de las cubiertas de Icaria).

Kolonihaven. Wooden House. Copenhagen. 1996

Architects/**Arquitectos:** Enric Miralles & Benedetta Tagliabue
Commission/**Encargo:** Fonden Kolonihaven. Kirsten Kiser
Project Team/**Equipo de proyecto:** Ricardo Flores, Fabián Asunción
Collaborators/**Colaboradores:** Elena Rocchi, Vibeke Linde Strandby,
Hernán Díaz Alonso, Leandro López, Caterina Miralles Tagliabue
Model/**Maqueta:** Fabián Asunción, Tom Broekaert
Photographs/**Fotografías:** Giovanni Zanzi

The Kolonihaven project invited different architects to design a house for a new development in Copenhagen. The invitation attempts to marry contemporary architecture to the Danish tradition of constructing, on the edges of the town, a small wooden house for leisure and gardening activities during the summer months. Benedetta Tagliabue and Enric Miralles thought of their work for Kolonihaven as a space that would reflect the passing of time: atmospheric and chronological time, and the transitoriness of both as manifested in the cultivation of flowers. To achieve this the house becomes a calendar which registers space, time and also the first steps of a child. In effect the architects proposed their scheme as a child's playroom into which the adult is invited, as in the Le Corbusier drawing, 'Papa, vient chez moi!' Built of wood, after maquettes made in soap, the house as a play space has different-sized doors for adults and children. The house's size, its irregular shape and its siting on a kind of dish transform it into a stone set within a landscape of bonsais. This, then, is to evoke, alongside the Nordic tradition, Japanese stone miniatures and gardens.

Kolonihaven. Casa de madera. Copenhague, 1996

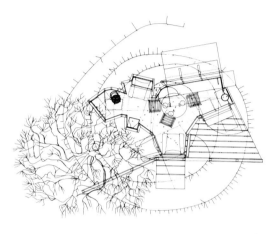

El proyecto Kolonihaven invitó a diferentes arquitectos a proponer un diseño de casa para un nuevo desarrollo en Copenhague. Dicha invitación trata de contemplar, desde la perspectiva de la arquitectura contemporánea, la tradición danesa de construir en las afueras de la ciudad un pequeño pabellón de madera en el que pasar los días del verano entre el ocio y las labores del jardín. Benedetta Tagliabue y Enric Miralles pensaron en su obra para Kolonihaven como en un espacio que reflejase el paso del tiempo: el atmosférico, el cronológico y la caducidad de ambos, que se manifiesta en el cultivo de las flores. De este modo, la casa se convierte en un calendario que da cuenta del espacio, el tiempo y, a la vez, los primeros pasos de un niño. De hecho, los arquitectos plantearon el proyecto como una habitación infantil a la que el adulto es invitado como en el dibujo de Le Corbusier: "Papa, vient chez moi!" Construida en madera a partir de maquetas de jabón, la casa como espacio de juego consta de una puerta para los adultos y otra para los niños, con sus alturas respectivas. Su tamaño, su forma irregular y su emplazamiento sobre un plato la convierten en una piedra dentro de un paisaje de bonsáis. Se trata, así, de evocar, junto a la tradición nórdica, las miniaturas de piedra y los jardines japoneses.

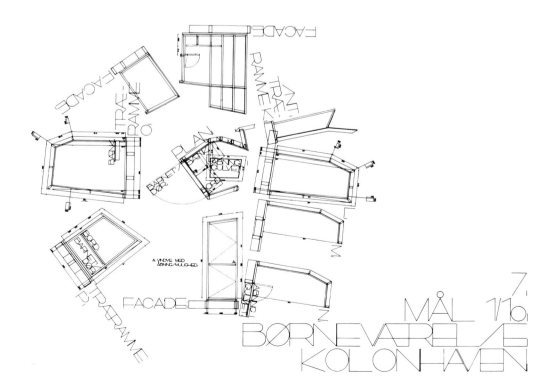

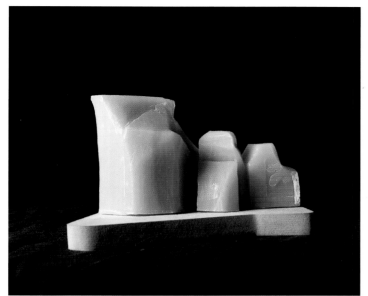

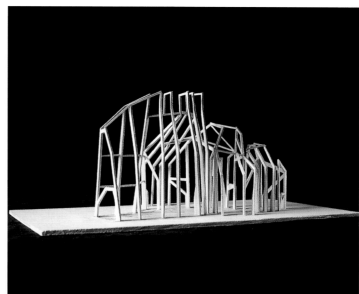

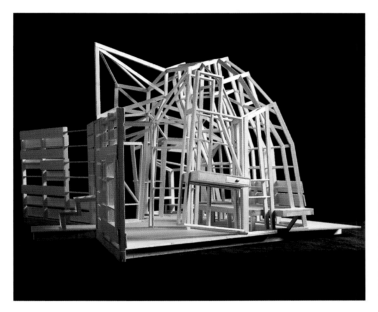

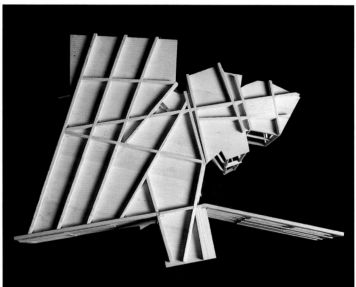

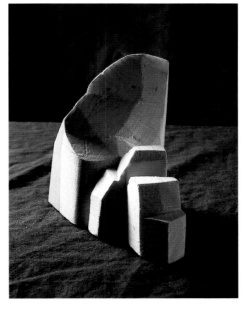

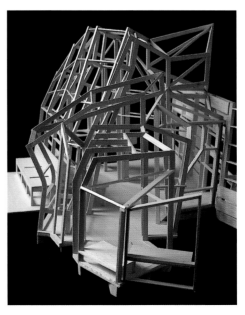

'Domus Totem'. Milan. 1998

Architect/**Arquitecto:** Enric Miralles & Benedetta Tagliabue
Project team/**Equipo de proyecto:** Joan Callis
Collaborators/**Colaboradores:** Hirotaka Koizumi,
Elena Rocchi, Karl Unglaubb
Sheet-metalworking/**Caldereria:** Delgado SA, Barcelona
Clockmaker/**Relojeros:** Perrot, Alemania
Structure/**Estructura**: Ove Arup, Steve Fisher, Daniele Bosia
Architect for Domus/**Arquitecto para Domus:** Luigi Spinelli

Invited to celebrate, by developing the idea of a totem, the 70th anniversary of the magazine *Domus*, Miralles and Tagliabue sited their contribution on the open space extending in front of Milan's Central Railroad Station. The work consists of three 15-meter-high uprights, topped by clocks on each of whose faces the hours, minutes and seconds are read separately. As well as inserting their Totem in the forest of posts populating the urban space, the architects endeavored to experiment to the full with different materials - stainless steel and titanium - in order to arrive at the greatest harmony possible between top and post, height and solidity, without sacrificing the movement provoked by the wind. This meant, moreover, that the project would be sited in the highly specific, even conflictive, zone defined by the immense station, the Pirelli Building, a wooded area and a vast wasteland. This space, then, is a sort of crossroads, a 'lobby' for the coming-and-going of many European travellers. Looked at that way the Totem, which is made up of identical objects with different movements, takes account of the city's rituals and the passing of time, and appears as one more traveller, one more migrant.

"Totem Domus". Milán, 1998

Invitados a celebrar, a partir de la idea de tótem, el 70º aniversario de la revista *Domus*, Miralles y Tagliabue instalaron su pieza en el gran espacio que se extiende frente a la Estación Central de Ferrocarril de Milán. La obra consta de tres mástiles de 15 m de altura coronados por sendos cuadrantes de reloj, de tal modo que la lectura de las horas, los minutos y los segundos ha de hacerse de modo independiente. Amén de insertar su Tótem en el bosque de postes que pueblan el espacio urbano, los arquitectos pretendían experimentar hasta el límite con diferentes materiales –de acero inoxidable a titanio– para conseguir la mayor armonía entre la cabeza y el mástil, la altura y la solidez sin renunciar al movimiento provocado por el viento. Por otro lado, se trataba de que este proyecto se asentase en una zona muy característica, conflictiva incluso, conformada por el inmenso edificio de la estación, el de Pirelli, una zona arbolada y un gran descampado. Este espacio es, pues, cruce de caminos, antesala de todos los viajes y acceso a Europa de muchos emigrantes. Desde este punto de vista, el Tótem, que está formado por objetos iguales con movimientos diferentes, da cuenta del ritual de la ciudad y del paso del tiempo, es como otro viajero que llega, un emigrante más.

'Abitare La Masieri'/'Living La Masieri'. Palazzeto Masieri. Venice. 1997

Architects/Arquitectos: Enric Miralles & Benedetta Tagliabue
Collaborators/Colaboradores: Elena Rocchi, Fabián Asunción

The installation planned for the Masieri Foundation, situated on the Foscari Canal but with views of the Grand Canal, occupied two of the palace floors, and set out to create a dialog between the architecture of Miralles-Tagliabue and the city of Venice. To do this the architects created a live-in space on the ground floor with a content and feeling similar to that expressed in the Barnola Gallery in Barcelona. The idea of the trip to Venice was, moreover, linked to that of habitability, and so the pieces formed part of a house intended to be moved and adapted to the place of arrival. Lastly, sculptures of Murano glass, the work of Mary Rosini, were combined with their own travelling works.

For its part, the upper floor of the Palazzeto Masieri was filled with giant drawings up to 11 meters long, installed within a small space and folded to form, in turn, a room. These drawings, which tried to recreate the feeling of vast Venetian School canvases, were covered with plexiglass, on which was reflected the outside of the building: the city itself and the Grand Canal.

'Abitare La Masieri'. Palazzeto Masieri. Venecia, 1997

La instalación proyectada para la Fundación Masieri, situada en el Canal Foscari pero con vistas al Gran Canal, ocupaba dos de las plantas del palacio y trataba de plantear un diálogo entre la arquitectura de Miralles-Tagliabue y la ciudad de Venecia. Para ello, los arquitectos crearon en la planta baja un espacio habitable con un espíritu y unos elementos similares a los empleados en la Galería Barnola de Barcelona. No obstante, a la idea de habitabilidad se unía la del viaje a Italia, con lo que las piezas formaban parte de una casa que debía trasladarse y adaptarse al lugar de llegada.

Finalmente, a sus trabajos viajeros se unieron esculturas de cristal de Murano obra de Mary Rosini.

Por su parte, la planta superior del Palazzeto Masieri fue ocupada por dibujos gigantes con perspectivas de hasta 11 metros que se instalaron en un pequeño espacio dentro del que se plegaban hasta formar, a su vez, una habitación. Estos dibujos, que trataban de recuperar la impresión de las grandes telas en las escuelas venecianas, iban cubiertos por plexiglás sobre el que se reflejaba el exterior del edificio: la propia ciudad y el Gran Canal.

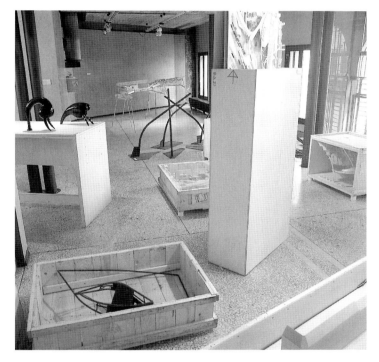

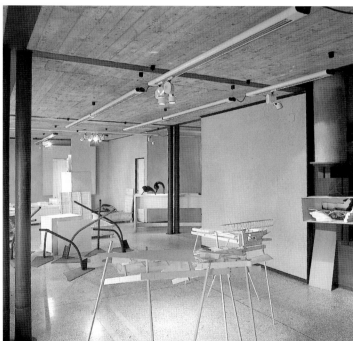

'Paseos'/'Walks'. Spanish Academy. Rome. 1995

In their project for the building in the Piazza de San Pietro in Montorio, Enric Miralles and Benedetta Tagliabue attempted to introduce the pergolas of the Olympic Village in Barcelona to a space marked by its proximity to such a work as Bramante's temple. Their intervention in the unroofed part of the Spanish Academy cloister consisted in erecting the iron structures of the Avenida Icaria on the lawn as if they were plants in a garden. With the help of the Academy's gardener the uprights, in fact, ended up as actual plants. Inside the cloister, on the other hand, the architects presented a somewhat abstract series of photo portraits that gave each of the 14 pergolas the look of a person. At the same time, and on another side of the patio quadrangle, a series of plexiglass half-cylinders similar to those used in Harvard in 1993 struck up a dialog with the columns of the cloister and, indirectly, with Bramante's work. A stroll along a Barcelona avenue was thus transposed to a walk through the Rome building, each wing of which was used in a different way.

'Paseos'. Academia de España. Roma, 1995

En su proyecto para el edificio de la Piazza de San Pietro in Montorio, Enric Miralles y Benedetta Tagliabue trataron de presentar las pérgolas de la Villa Olímpica barcelonesa en un espacio marcado por la vecindad con una obra como el templete de Bramante. La intervención en la zona descubierta del claustro de la Academia de España consistió en plantar en el césped los hierros de la avenida Icaria como si se tratase de plantas del jardín. De hecho, los mástiles terminaron convirtiéndose en tales plantas con la colaboración del jardinero de la academia. Por otro lado, en el interior del claustro,

los arquitectos presentaron la serie, en principio abstracta, de las 14 pérgolas a través de 14 retratos fotográficos que daban a cada una de ellas un tratamiento de personaje figurativo. Al mismo tiempo, y en un lado distinto del cuadrado del patio, una serie de semicilindros de plexiglás, similares a los usados en Harvard en 1993, entablaban un diálogo con las columnas del claustro e, indirectamente, con la obra de Bramante. De este modo, se trasladaba el paseo por la avenida barcelonesa al paseo por el edificio romano, cada una de cuyas alas era empleada de modo diferente.

'Heaven'. Tateyama Museum-Park. Japan. 1994-95

Architect/**Arquitecto:** Enric Miralles
Local architect/**Arquitecto local:** Kijo Rokakku Archs
Collaborators/**Colaboradores:** Julie Rouault,
Monique Buretta, Ana Poyuelo

Belonging to his research into the material nature of seemingly immaterial phenomena like light or the human, Enric Miralles caused both representation and construction to coincide in this work. The architect attempted, basically, to lend density to the light inside a small concrete volume. He accordingly tried to materialize the human dimension by means of a series of curved metal shapes which received and reflected the light from above. The progressive ageing of the copper, furthermore, gave the design an inescapably temporal aspect.
This work responded to an invitation to design, for the garden of a sort of theme park, a building that would depict heaven or paradise, hence the title. Figuratively speaking, Miralles' intervention consisted in creating the model of a cloud whose three dimensions grow out of variations in the way its strata change in section. The overhead light, a kind of sun, was reflected in a mirror, thus creating a virtual space that duplicated the real play of light and shadow.

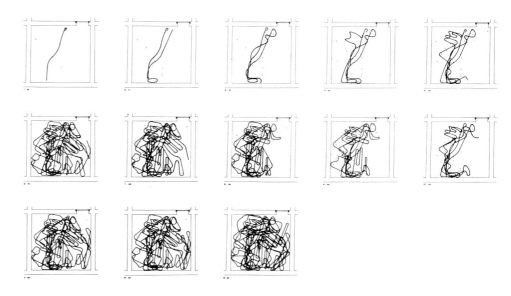

'Heaven'. Parque-museo de Tateyama, Japón. 1995

Dentro de una investigación sobre la materialidad de fenómenos en principio inmateriales como la luz o lo humano, Enric Miralles hizo coincidir en este trabajo representación y construcción. El arquitecto intentaba, básicamente, otorgar densidad a la luz dentro de un pequeño volumen de cemento. Así mismo, trató de materializar la dimensión humana a través de una serie de perfiles de metal curvado sobre los que se extendía y se reflejaba la luz cenital. El envejecimiento progresivo del cobre concedía al proyecto un ineludible matiz temporal.

Este trabajo respondía a una invitación para proyectar, en el jardín de una suerte de parque temático, un pabellón que representase el cielo-paraíso, de ahí su título. Figurativamente el intento consistía en crear la maqueta de una nube cuyas tres dimensiones surgían mediante variaciones de estratos al cambiar de sección. La luz cenital, a modo de sol, se reflejaba en un espejo creando un espacio virtual que duplicaba el juego real de claridad y sombra.

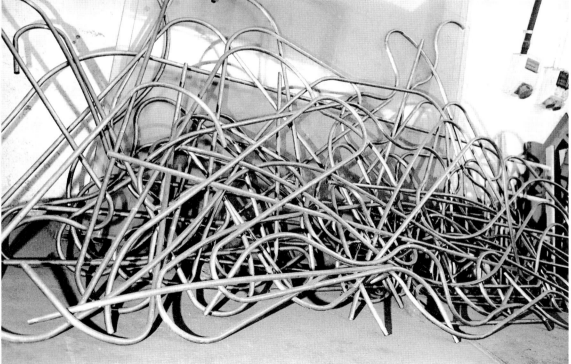

Miralles Tagliabue
Time architecture

It's in temporary projects, in more ephemeral architectures, that Enric Miralles finds greatest creative freedom. Exhibitions and stands, installations and décors thus go to form the more personal terrain and most frequent typology in his partnership with Benedetta Tagliabue. Miralles speaks of temporary architecture over time, of the life of time in architecture. Time as modifier, as variant and ultimately as response, is, he asserts, the final arbiter in an architect's work.

Do you think each time has its own architecture? Each period its own art?

For me time has to do with the journey, and the journey to do with movement. Once, while presenting us in Japan, Arata Isozaki called us *marevitos*. *Marevitos* translates as 'actor'. These were old-time puppeteers who, as well as taking a theater show from village to village, also carried the news, the latest, from one place to another. What interests me about itinerant artists is such movement. They arrived in villages, left a few things, took other things away. That idea of movement and time is what interests me about ephemeral architecture.

Does the role of the architect as messenger interest you?

I'm interested in being aware at all times that this kind of architecture can be a game which nevertheless leaves a trace. We often work blind due to wanting to do things, to getting the most out of the means we have. In reality that's what we are, agents between different places. Before things happen you have to imagine them; for that reason the rela-

tionship between the journey, construction and information is something consubstantial with architecture.

Aside from the message, the journey itself interests me. The journey in architecture is a very wide term. My doctoral thesis, *Things Seen to Left and Right*, was a reflection on travel notebooks prior to the French Revolution. I was interested in the type of journey that has to do with learning. In time you realize about the narrow relation that exists between the journey, movement, learning and the profession of architect. Architects carry ideas from one place to another. We are, in effect, messengers.

Today, with the means that exist to know about other cultures without needing to visit them, wouldn't yours be a somewhat nostalgic view of the profession of architect?

Without journeying, without movement, there's no change; and more than visiting Hamburg in Hamburg and Japan in Japan, I'm interested in combining them and in seeking the one in the other. You can only do that by going off to those places.

Pergolas. Avenida Icaria, Olimpic Village. Barcelona'92.

Why go looking for things and places precisely where they're not?

It's crass to doubt that you'll find Japan in Japan. It's more difficult to find it where it supposedly isn't, and yet it does appear in buildings, in influences. The shifting of the exhibition of studio works is something we do ourselves, like anybody moving house. Exhibitions, in fact, work like that: you take the place they give you to work in and transform it into a place to live in. We use the exhibition space as an exercise in living. We believe that the way we install ourselves in a new space says more about the projects themselves than any book or video could ever do. We speak about our projects, demonstrating what our experience of space is, and it's that experience we're interested in communicating through our ephemeral installations.

Then, a time-based architecture would exploit the temporal dimension in the abstract, without necessarily pertaining to a particular period.

Something like that, at least in the historical sense.

Architects **carry ideas** from one place to another. We are, in effect, **messengers.**

The 20th century is a period of distinct times. Due to the speed and ease of information, the historical notion of time as immanence has become confused with real time. This century has lived the idea of time from the atemporality that the Modern Movement supposed and from the quoting of other epochs. The constant recuperation of moments from the past is one of the characteristics of the architecture of the 20th century.

And its failure too, maybe?

Well..., I wouldn't go that far.

In architecture the borrowing of styles has rarely worked in the long term.

In the long term, no, but like that thing called life it's something to be getting along with... Modernity sus- tains the so-called avant-garde. In this century, when Eisenman quotes Terragni, it works. When Koolhaas, say what you like, bases his designs on different Le Corbusier projects, it works. When Gardella quotes the elegant architecture of the 19th century, it works. And the same thing happens with Asplund or Rossi.

The architectural avant-garde is a book of quotes, then?

It would be extremely difficult to come up with a conceptual scheme in the architecture of this century that didn't have its origins in an earlier work.

Why is it that literal, direct quotations never work?

Because the architecture that copies will never have the intensity of that which it copied. It's not a question of copying, but of incorporating, assimilating. When you identify yourself with something, that something is converted into a kind of ghost and you put yourself in its body. In repeating the gestures of a place or a person, one is incorporated by them. There's a wonderful text by Javier Marías called *The Ghost of Saint Stephen* [in fact the story is called *The Resignation of Saint Stephen*, but Miralles has retained the idea of the ghost] which talks about a house in which noises are heard and doors open by themselves. The story describes perfectly that idea of repetition when on a certain day, at a particular hour, in a precise room, the owner of the house does exactly what he knows the ghost will do. That's why I don't think the quoting of styles is a disaster. It certainly isn't from the individual point of view and as an intellectual option. The moment that those quotations turn into a style that society has to live with, the thing changes, because society isn't in the mood for stories and has other kinds of problems to solve before getting around to recognizing the rebirth of a style.

Do you think it would be a sign of cultural health if society were to reject the labels which styles borrow?

I think it already rejects them as a social phenomenon. Nevertheless, as a personal option, the quotation, the incorporation of other kinds of knowledge, is an alternative it's difficult to avoid. One learns through repetition, through absorption and through incorporation.

If, as you say, architecture doesn't have its time, its moment, how then does it change? How does one style succeed another? What determines architecture, if not time?

Yes, it possesses time, but a relative, fluctuating time. It takes a lot to realize that the sense of time is a material that's part and parcel of architecture; that's to say, having the same importance as bricks. The need for destruction that weighs heavily on certain built works forms part of this relationship to time. There are public spaces, green areas that, when building a city for example, have ceased to exist, have been transformed. Destruction is a speeding up of time, and building is too, in effect. The solution to getting in touch with time is to not make things that are indestructible.

Don't you think that the most important thing about architecture is its permanence?

I think it's more important to learn to navigate in time and to work with it consciously.

It would be extremely difficult to come up
with a **conceptual scheme** in the architecture
of this century that didn't have its origins
in an **earlier work.**

Wouldn't permanence be another way, albeit illusory, to manipulate time?

Permanence is contrary to existence. Things are forever changing. As a student I was very interested in Rossi's ideas because they were able to give me enormous freedom of variation. If you have a sort of temporal structure that you could summarize in the foundations of a building, you know that ultimately the foundations are always there to play with, and you have the freedom to vary things. In fact you realize that these foundations don't exist, and that they're the variants, the constant modifications of the ideas, schemes and notions that go to give architecture its density.

I'm not at all concerned with the image or the texture of volumes or materials. I'm more concerned with the logic of the dimensions. One overdoes it with the materials. There are four materials for building a work –steel, stone, glass and little more– that can be made more or less transparent. What gives architecture character is the space and the content one gives to a project.

And what for you is the content that one gives to a project?

In my more recent works I use the technique and experience I've gradually acquired from my previous projects to experiment with different content. In the projects for exhibitions, in temporary architectures, I explore the idea of the journey. Through the journey you arrive at the idea of variations and you learn that these are as important as the final result.

Are the variations, the changes, decisive in your projects?

In almost all, yes they are, and definitively so in these types of assignments. The end result is no more than a more defined vibration that grows out of all the changes there have been between the initial project and the final construction. In its very formation architecture incorporates the idea of the journey, of the variable. And so it seems fitting to me that the forms incorporate this idea of the variable.

In the competition for the Scottish Parliament the basic idea was to come up with a building capable of representing a people. It was important for us that the architecture reflect the fact that the members of parliament were part of an organized society and that it did this without recourse to the transparencies that would convert the building into a huge fishbowl. That was the challenge and our main argument for settling on the design.

That's an idea that's much more conceptual than architectonic.

No, that's just where the mistake lies. Because as an architect I have to apply all I know of tradition, of building techniques, in order to construct an idea.

I'm referring to the fact that your initial idea isn't a form.

It's the origin of the form. Once one has a valid idea, the form follows.

But it's an undefined form, a form obtained through negation, in deciding what one doesn't want to do.

That's the most important thing in architecture: to be clear about what it is one doesn't want to do in each project. What it is you want to do you gradually find out and slowly it emerges. The variations I was talking about earlier are what decide a design.

You start from a formless idea which gradually takes on form during the construction process.

Exactly.

What guarantee do you have that the citizen will interpret the ensuing form in accordance with your initial intentions?

I think the citizens make that elementary reading right away. How, depends on each design. The Scottish Parliament, for instance, relates to the landscape by means of a number of situations that could well be an open-ended mimicry of all that happens in the parliament.

There's something in the behavior of the individual, in body language, in the way of relating, that at a certain point fuses the civic use and the architecture, and it's there that the design is finalized. I think that the paved squares of Barcelona, for example, were basically an intuitive thing. Nobody could predict what the social behavior related to those squares would be.

Who or what, do you think, has to do the adapting: the space to the people or the people to the space?

That's something complex, open and, furthermore, mutual. Things and people affect each other mutually. It's important to use architecture as an instrument for exploring new kinds of relationships. When the architecture is built, the use the citizens make of it often supposes new variations, and those variations continue being a journey that keeps the architecture alive.

In your temporary works you become a kind of narrator who explains the exhibitions.

My most personal work explores issues that are semi-secret and therefore difficult to communicate. In the public and exhibition works it's crucial for me to be able to communicate with the users, and naturally I do that using the language I know. In the project for the Icaria pergolas, for instance, the idea of the umbracle and the walkway is combined with that of the big annual festival, the idea of the timbers and the landscape of palm trees with that of a procession of carnival figures and giants.

Are you saying that the initial ideas, the concepts you were describing at the beginning, don't have to be architectonic ideas, that they can be experiences, for example?

They usually are. Sometimes subjective ones, sometimes social. I think that the greater part of the ideas we have are not ours. They form part of a sort of spirit of the times. The spirit of a particular time is shaped more by critical ability, the ability a society has to interpret, than by the forms of architects.

For that reason, it isn't easy to work within that spirit.

Do you think that socio-cultural factors are more important in defining architecture than formal or technical questions?

Yes. Right now we're working on a project for a golf club in the Cerdanya. The landscape factors are so important that we decided to do a scheme which was totally integrated into the location until we suddenly realized that we ought to also take on board the idea that golf is a communal thing. There lay our challenge as architects: trying to build in a landscape by creating another viable landscape, capable of responding to and agreeing with a community of users.

Where does an architect get social information of that sort?

From observation and documentation. And they don't just serve historical purposes, because it's a question of going back and listening to people. Typologies cease to have importance, because one must listen to the user and understand his current needs. Such information will be what decides the project, knowledge will be what builds it. As an architect I recognize a technique that permits me to think. Through architecture itself I learn to make architecture, and there's a moment in which you step outside that way of working and start to fix on other things. I've done many marginal jobs which I suppose I got from people who knew how to recognize that objective in my architecture.

For example?

In Japan they commissioned me to do a pavilion for meditating in, when it's certain there were many architects there better equipped than me to do it.

So to what do you attribute such commissions?

In the same way that I use architecture, the knowledge I've gradually acquired, to investigate things, the person who takes a chance on the architect is the person who hands out the commission. Isozaki gave me that job with certain precise objectives in mind.

My architecture **explores** the idea of the **journey.**

Does the degree of experimentation vary when the architecture isn't ephemeral?

Long-term architecture is more organized, it has to be. Our architecture has always interpreted the location, and that's something temporary works of architecture make apparent. In them, the response is usually rapid and open-ended, and you often have to construct an unstable architecture in places of varying size. In that sense temporary architectures are compact, immediate and adaptable.

Could it be said that your most intuitive works are those that are the least worked?

Due to design and time limits you can permit yourself the sort of boldness that would be out of place in other buildings. An architect, though, experiments throughout his professional career. Experiment is linked to how long your life lasts, not to how long your buildings do. I've always admired Louis Kahn's work. The great thing about him is that he didn't have time to test anything, but he possessed intuition and he followed it. Le Corbusier had time, tested things, so that the buildings after Chandigarh constitute a critique of Chandigarh itself.

That occurs in the work of a lot of painters.

But it's not the same, because painting has other limits, different execution times that are faster and much more stable. If we could 'read' Kahn, his work would be most like Proust's: gestures that are closed in on themselves, part memory, part intuition... Very few architects have been capable of doing something similar.

On the one hand you speak of architecture's need to be convivial, and on the other you admire the work of an architect you take to be Proustian, consumed by memory...

We architects speak like strategists, we speak of things that may or may not happen. We don't speak using criteria of truth. You try and pursue your calling in the most coherent and honorable way you can, yet you go on trying things out. What interests me is that the testings bear the weight of a more complex thinking.

What determines the form of a building?

The form of a building doesn't concern me in the least.

But surely your clients like to know what it is they're commissioning?

They know, but not from the facade.

Did the building that's won the Edinburgh Parliament competition win it without a defined image?

If a person isn't worried about the forms, the architecture acquires enormous formal freedom. There's something beyond the sort of decorum that, from the word go, is very important for some architects and which, for me, only becomes so right at the end. I like to think using more abstract terms like scale, the container and other questions.

Questions like the movement of the users and the spaces that result from this?

Let's not delude ourselves. The Dutch are now talking about the movement of the masses as if this were something new, without quoting the sources they got those ideas from, ideas which are basic to the vocabulary of Guy Debord. There's a strategy which consists in postponing things, in not deciding anything apart from what they ask you for. We architects are in the habit of deciding everything, and at times this isn't necessary and at others it's even better not to. Melville wrote a story called *Bartleby the Scrivener* in which the main character is an office worker who responds to everything they ask of him with "I'd rather not". We architects should learn from him and grant other temporalities to architecture.

Anatxu Zabalbeascoa

Miralles Tagliabue
Arquitecturas del tiempo

En los proyectos temporales, en las arquitecturas más efímeras, es donde mayor libertad creativa encuentra Enric Miralles.

Las exposiciones y los *stands*, las instalaciones y los decorados conforman, así mismo, el terreno más íntimo y la tipología más frecuente en su asociación con Benedetta Tagliabue. Miralles habla de la arquitectura temporal a través del tiempo, de la vida del tiempo en la arquitectura. El tiempo como modificador, como variante y, finalmente, como respuesta es –asegura– el responsable final de los proyectos de un arquitecto.

¿Cree que existe una arquitectura de cada tiempo, un arte de cada época?

Para mí el tiempo tiene que ver con el viaje, y el viaje con el movimiento. Una vez, al presentarnos en Japón, Arata Isozaki habló de nosotros como de *marevitos*. *Marevitos* se traduciría por comediantes. Eran los titiriteros antiguos que, además de trasladar una representación teatral de pueblo en pueblo, en su desplazamiento llevaban también las noticias, lo novedoso de un lugar a otro. Lo que me interesa de los artistas ambulantes es ese movimiento. Llegaban a los pueblos para dejar unas cosas y se llevaban otras. Esa idea de movimiento y tiempo es la que me interesa de la arquitectura efímera.

¿Le interesa el papel del arquitecto como mensajero?

Me interesa tener consciencia en todo momento de que este tipo de arquitectura puede ser un juego que, sin embargo, deja huella. Muchas veces trabajamos cegados por querer hacer las cosas, por sacar partido a los medios que tenemos. En realidad somos eso, agentes entre distintos lugares. Antes de que sucedan las cosas debes imaginarlas, por eso la relación entre el viaje, la construcción y la información es algo consustancial a la arquitectura.

Además del mensaje, me interesa el viaje. El viaje en arquitectura es un término muy amplio. Mi tesis doctoral *Cosas vistas a izquierda y derecha* era una reflexión sobre los cuadernos de viaje anteriores a la Revolución Francesa. Me interesaba la variante del viaje que tiene que ver con el aprendizaje. Con el tiempo te das cuenta de la estrecha relación que existe entre el viaje, el movimiento, el aprendizaje y nuestra profesión de arquitecto. Los arquitectos cargamos ideas de un lugar para otro. Somos, efectivamente, mensajeros.

Hoy en día, con los medios que existen para conocer otras culturas sin necesidad de visitarlas, ¿no sería la suya una visión algo nostálgica de la profesión de arquitecto?

Sin viaje, sin movimiento, no hay traslado y, a mí, más que visitar Hamburgo en Hamburgo y Japón en Japón, me interesa combinarlos y buscarlos unos en otros. Eso sólo lo puedes hacer trasladándote hasta esos lugares.

¿Para qué buscar las cosas y los lugares donde no están?

Es muy tonto dudar de que encontrarás Japón en Japón. Es más difícil encontrarlo donde supuestamente no está y, sin embargo, aparece en construcciones, en influencias.

El traslado de la exposición de los trabajos del estudio nosotros lo hacemos como quien realiza una mudanza. De hecho, las exposiciones funcionan así: se coge el lugar que te dan para trabajar y se transforma en un lugar para habitar. Utilizamos el lugar de exposición como un ejercicio de habitación. Al mostrar nuestros propios proyectos, cree-

Los arquitectos **cargamos ideas** de un lugar para otro. Somos, efectivamente, **mensajeros.**

mos que la manera de instalarnos en un nuevo espacio habla más de los proyectos en sí que todo cuanto los libros y los vídeos pueden llegar a explicar. Hablamos de nuestros proyectos demostrando cuál es nuestra experiencia del espacio, y es esa experiencia lo que nos interesa transmitir con nuestros montajes efímeros.

Entonces, para usted, una arquitectura del tiempo trabajaría la dimensión temporal en abstracto, sin pertenecer necesariamente a una época.

Algo así, por lo menos en el sentido histórico. El siglo XX es una época de tiempos distintos. Debido a la velocidad y a la facilidad de información, la idea histórica del tiempo como devenir se ha confundido con el tiempo real. Este siglo ha vivido la idea de tiempo desde la atemporalidad que supuso el movimiento moderno y desde la cita de otras épocas.

La constante recuperación de momentos del pasado es una de las características de la arquitectura del siglo XX.

¿Y tal vez también su fracaso?

Bueno..., no diría yo tanto.

En arquitectura, la recuperación de estilos rara vez ha funcionado a largo plazo.

A largo plazo no, pero como esto de la vida es sólo para ir tirando… La modernidad alimenta a la supuesta vanguardia. Dentro del siglo, cuando Eisenman recupera a Terragni, le funciona. Cuando Koolhaas, diga lo que diga, diseña a partir de algunos proyectos de Le Corbusier, le funciona. Cuando Gardella recupera la arquitectura culta del XIX, le funciona. Y lo mismo sucede con Asplund o Rossi…

¿La vanguardia arquitectónica es un libro de citas?

Sería muy difícil dar con una operación conceptual en la arquitectura de este siglo que no tuviese las raíces puestas en un trabajo anterior.

¿Por qué las recuperaciones literales directas nunca funcionan?

Porque la arquitectura que copia no tendrá nunca la fuerza de lo que copió. No se trata de copiar, sino de incorporar, de asimilar. Cuando te identificas con algo, ese algo se convierte en una especie de fantasma y te metes en su propio cuerpo. Uno se incorpora repitiendo los gestos de un lugar o de una persona.

Hay un texto muy bonito de Javier Marías que se llama *El fantasma de Santiesteban* (en realidad, el cuento se llama *La dimisión de Santiesteban*, pero Miralles ha retenido la idea del fantasma) que habla

sobre una casa en la que se oyen unos ruidos, se abren unas puertas. El cuento explica perfectamente esa idea de la repetición cuando un determinado día, a una hora concreta, en una habitación precisa, el propietario de la casa hace aquello que sabe que hará el fantasma. Por eso mismo, no me parece que la recuperación de estilos sea un fracaso. No lo es desde el punto de vista individual y como opción intelectual. En el momento en que esas recuperaciones se convierten en un estilo que debe asumir la sociedad, la cosa cambia, porque la sociedad no está para cuentos y tiene otro tipo de problemas que solucionar antes de ponerse a reconocer el renacimiento de un estilo.

¿Cree que sería un signo de salud cultural el hecho de que la sociedad rechazara las etiquetas que recuperan los estilos?

Yo creo que ya las rechaza como fenómeno social. Sin embargo, como opción personal, la cita histórica, la incorporación de otros saberes, es una alternativa difícil de evitar. Se aprende por repetición, por absorción o por incorporación.

Si, como dice, la arquitectura no tiene un tiempo, un momento, ¿Cómo cambia entonces? ¿Cómo se suceden los estilos? ¿Qué determina la arquitectura que no sea el tiempo?

Sí tiene tiempo, pero tiempo relativo, fluctual. Ya es mucho darse cuenta de que el sentido del tiempo es un material que forma parte de la arquitectura consustancialmente, es decir, con la misma importancia que los ladrillos. No se trata de entender el tiempo como duración. La necesidad de destrucción que pesa sobre algunas obras construidas forma parte de esta relación con el tiempo. Hay espacios públicos, zonas verdes que para construir una ciudad, por ejemplo, han dejado de existir, se han transformado. La destrucción es una aceleración del tiempo, y el construir, en realidad, también lo es. La solución para relacionarse con el tiempo no es hacer cosas indestructibles.

¿No le parece que lo más importante de la arquitectura sea la permanencia?

Me parece más importante aprender a navegar en el tiempo y trabajar con él conscientemente.

¿La permanencia no sería otra manera, tal vez ilusoria, de trabajar el tiempo?

La permanencia es contraria a la existencia. Las cosas se modifican continuamente. A mí, como estudiante, me interesaba mucho el pensamiento de Rossi porque me abría una enorme libertad de variación. Si tienes una especie de estructura temporal que podrías resumir en los cimientos de un edificio, sabes que al final siempre están los cimientos para jugar con ellos, para tener la libertad de variar las cosas. En la realidad te das cuenta de que estos cimientos no existen, de que son las variantes, la constante modificación de las ideas, de los pro-

Pérgolas. Avenida Icaria, Villa Olímpica. Barcelona '92.

Sería muy difícil dar con una **operación conceptual** en la **arquitectura de este siglo** que no tuviese las **raíces** puestas en un **trabajo anterior.**

yectos y de las condiciones, lo que va dando a la arquitectura su densidad.

No estoy nada preocupado por la imagen o la textura de los volúmenes o los materiales. Me preocupa más la lógica de las dimensiones. Con los materiales se exagera mucho. Para construir una obra hay cuatro materiales –acero, piedra, cristal y poco más– que se pueden hacer más o menos transparentes. Lo que da cara a la arquitectura es el espacio y el contenido que se le da a un proyecto.

¿Y qué es para usted el contenido que se le da a un proyecto?

En mis últimos trabajos utilizo la técnica y la experiencia que he ido adquiriendo con mis proyectos anteriores para experimentar con los contenidos. En los proyectos para exposiciones, en las arquitecturas temporales, investigo la idea del viaje. A través del viaje te acercas a la idea de las variaciones y aprendes que éstas son tan importantes como el resultado final.

¿Las variaciones, los cambios, son determinantes en sus proyectos?

En casi todos sí, y definitivamente sí en este tipo de encargos. El resultado último no es más que una vibración más definida que resulta de todos los cambios habidos desde el proyecto inicial hasta la construcción final. La arquitectura incorpora, en su formación, la idea del viaje, de lo variable. De ahí

que me parezca apropiado que las formas incorporen esta idea de lo variable. En el concurso para el Parlamento de Escocia, una idea fundamental fue la de encontrar un edificio capaz de representar a un pueblo. Nos parecía importante que la arquitectura reflejase que los parlamentarios eran parte de una sociedad organizada y que lo hiciese sin recurrir a las transparencias que convertirían el edificio en una gran pecera. Ese fue nuestro reto y nuestro principal argumento para decidir el diseño.

Se trata de una idea mucho más conceptual que arquitectónica.

No, ahí está el error. Porque como arquitecto tengo que aplicar cuanto conozco de tradición, de técnicas constructivas, para llegar a construir una idea.

Me refiero a que su idea inicial no es una forma.

Es la raíz de la forma, una vez se tiene una idea válida, la forma viene detrás.

Pero es una forma indefinida, obtenida de los negativos, de decidir lo que no se quiere hacer.

Eso es lo más importante en arquitectura: tener claro lo que no se quiere hacer con cada proyecto. Lo que quieres hacer lo vas averiguando y va saliendo. Las variaciones que antes comentaba son las que deciden el proyecto.

Usted parte de una idea informe que va adquiriendo forma en el proceso constructivo.

Exactamente.

¿Qué le asegura que el ciudadano interpretará la forma resultante de acuerdo con sus intenciones iniciales?

Creo que los ciudadanos hacen inmediatamente esa lectura elemental. El cómo depende de cada proyecto. El Parlamento escocés, por ejemplo, se relaciona con el paisaje a través de unas situaciones que podrían ser una mímica dialogante de cuanto sucede en el Parlamento. Hay algo en el proceder del individuo, en el lenguaje corporal, en la manera de relacionarse, que en determinado punto funde el uso ciudadano con la arquitectura, y ahí queda finalizado el proyecto. Creo que las plazas duras de Barcelona, por ejemplo, fueron, fundamentalmente, una operación de intuición. Nadie podía prever cuál sería el comportamiento social ligado a esas plazas.

¿Quién cree que se tenía que adaptar a quién: el espacio a la gente o la gente al espacio?

Eso es algo complejo, abierto y, además, mutuo. Las cosas y las personas se afectan mutuamente. Es importante utilizar la arquitectura como instrumento para explorar nuevas formas de relación. Cuando la arquitectura está construida, el uso que le dan los ciudadanos supone, muchas veces, nuevas variaciones, y esas variaciones siguen siendo un viaje que mantiene viva la arquitectura.

En sus trabajos temporales, se convierte en una especie de narrador que explica las exposiciones.

Mi trabajo más personal investiga cuestiones casi secretas y, por lo tanto, de difícil comunicación. En los trabajos públicos y expositivos es fundamental poder comunicarme con los usuarios, y eso, naturalmente, lo hago desde el lenguaje que yo conozco. En el proyecto de las pérgolas de Icaria, por ejemplo, se mezcla la idea del umbráculo y el paseo con la de la fiesta mayor, la idea de las maderas y el paisaje de palmeras con la de una procesión de cabezudos y gigantes.

¿Quiere decir que las primeras ideas, los conceptos que describía al principio, no tienen por qué ser ideas arquitectónicas, pueden ser vivencias, por ejemplo?

Suelen serlo. A veces subjetivas y a veces sociales. Creo que la mayor parte de las ideas que tenemos no son nuestras. Forman parte de una especie de espíritu de un tiempo. El espíritu de un tiempo viene dado más por la capacidad crítica, la capacidad de interpretar de una sociedad, que por las formas de los arquitectos. Por eso no es fácil trabajar dentro de ese espíritu.

¿Cree que los condicionantes socioculturales marcan la arquitectura por encima de cuestiones formales o técnicas?

Sí. Nosotros trabajamos ahora en un proyecto para un club de golf en la Cerdanya. Los condicionantes paisajísticos son tan grandes que decidimos hacer un proyecto totalmente integrado en el lugar hasta que, de repente, caímos en que debíamos de interpretar también la idea que una comunidad tiene del golf . Ahí estaba nuestro reto como arquitectos: en tratar de construir en un paisaje creando otro paisaje creíble capaz de responder y poner de acuerdo a una comunidad de usuarios.

¿De dónde saca la información social de ese tipo un arquitecto?

De la observación y la documentación. No sirven únicamente los usos históricos porque se trata de volver a entender a la gente. Las tipologías dejan de tener importancia porque se debe escuchar al usuario y comprender sus nuevas necesidades. Esa información será la que decidirá el proyecto, el conocimiento será lo que lo construirá. Como arquitecto conozco una técnica que me permite pensar. A través de la propia arquitectura aprendo a hacer

arquitectura, y hay un momento en el que das un paso al margen de ese proceder y te empiezas a fijar en otras cosas. He realizado muchos encargos marginales que supongo que me han llegado de gente que ha sabido leer ese objetivo en mi arquitectura.

¿Por ejemplo?

En Japón me encargaron un pabellón para la meditación cuando seguro que allí había muchísimos arquitectos más preparados que yo para hacerlo.

¿Y a qué atribuye esos encargos?

De la misma manera que utilizo la arquitectura, los conocimientos que he ido adquiriendo, para investigar, el que experimenta con el arquitecto es el que hace el encargo. Isozaki me hizo ese encargo con unos objetivos precisos.

¿El grado de experimentación varía cuando la arquitectura no es efímera?

La arquitectura de plazos largos es, necesariamente, más organizada. Nuestra arquitectura siempre ha interpretado el lugar, y eso lo transparentan los trabajos de arquitectura temporal. En ellos la respuesta suele ser rápida y amplia y, muchas veces, debes construir una arquitectura inestable en lugares de tamaño variable. En ese sentido, las arquitecturas temporales son densas, inmediatas y adaptables.

¿Se podría decir que son sus trabajos más intuitivos, los menos manipulados?

Por los plazos de diseño y duración te puedes permitir osadías que en otros edificios estarían fuera de lugar. Pero un arquitecto experimenta a lo largo de toda su trayectoria profesional. El experimento está ligado a la duración de tu vida, no a la duración de tus edificios. Siempre he admirado la obra de Louis Kahn. Lo bonito de su caso es que no tuvo tiempo de comprobar nada, pero tuvo intuición y la siguió. Le Corbusier tuvo tiempo, comprobó cosas y, así, los edificios posteriores a Chandigarh constituyen una crítica del propio Chandigarh.

Eso ocurre con la obra de muchos pintores.

Pero no es lo mismo, porque la pintura tiene otros plazos, otros tiempos mucho más rápidos de ejecución y mucho más estables en el tiempo. Si pudiéramos leer a Kahn, su trabajo sería lo más parecido a Proust: gestos encerrados en sí mismos, parte memoria, parte intuición... Muy pocos arqui-

tectos han sido capaces de realizar un ejercicio similar.

Por una parte habla de la necesidad de sociabilidad de la arquitectura y por otra admira el trabajo de un arquitecto que juzga proustiano, devorado por la memoria...

Los arquitectos hablamos como estrategas, hablamos de cosas que pueden suceder o no. No hablamos con criterios de verdad. Procuras desarrollar tu profesión lo más coherente y honradamente que puedes, pero vas comprobando cosas. Me interesa que las pruebas se agraven con un pensamiento más complejo.

¿Qué determina la forma de un edificio?

No me preocupa en absoluto la forma de un edificio.

Pero seguramente a sus clientes les gustará saber qué están encargando.

Lo saben, pero no por la fachada.

¿El edificio que ha ganado el Parlamento de Edimburgo lo ganó sin una imagen definida?

Si uno se despreocupa de las formas, la arquitectura gana una enorme libertad formal. Hay algo más allá de esta especie de decoro que para algunos arquitectos es muy importante desde el principio y que, para mí, sólo lo será al final. Me gusta pensar desde términos más abstractos como la escala, la envolvente y otras cuestiones.

¿Cuestiones como el movimiento de los usuarios y los espacios que resultan?

No nos engañemos. Los holandeses hablan ahora del movimiento de las masas como quien descubre algo, sin citar las fuentes de dónde sacaron esas ideas, que son fundamentales en el vocabulario de Guy Debord.

Hay una estrategia que consiste en posponer las cosas, en no decidir nada más que aquello que te piden. Los arquitectos tenemos la manía de decidirlo todo, y muchas veces no es necesario y otras es mejor no hacerlo. Melville tiene un cuento llamado *Bartleby el escribiente* en el que el protagonista es un oficinista que a todo lo que le piden responde: "Preferiría no hacerlo". Los arquitectos deberíamos aprender de él y dar a la arquitectura otros tiempos.

Anatxu Zabalbeascoa.

The Beauty of Stone
The Westminster Cathedral Marbles

The Beauty of Stone
The Westminster Cathedral Marbles

Patrick Rogers

First published 2008 by Oremus - The Magazine of Westminster Cathedral

Editor: Fr Tim Dean
Managing Editor: Blandine Tugendhat
Design and Art Direction: Julian Game

British Library Cataloguing-in-Publication Data

A catalogue record for this book is available from the British Library

ISBN 978-0-9560211-0-6

Printed in England by Aaron Printing Limited

Contents

FOREWORD

Anyone who enters Westminster Cathedral is bound to be struck by the variety and beauty of the marbles used in its decoration. Cardinal Vaughan had the idea of erecting a church whose structure could be completed quickly, whereas the decoration could be left until later. In Bentley's Byzantine scheme this would mostly take the form of marble and mosaic. Although the mosaics are far from complete, the marbles are, to all intents and purposes.

Some are identified in the various histories and guides, but until Patrick Rogers got to work there was no complete and authoritative list. Mgr Francis Bartlett, whose distinguished career at the Cathedral ended with his retirement as Administrator in 1977, was an expert, but, although urged to record his knowledge for posterity, never did so in detail. His brother Aelred, whose heroic and self-effacing work in the nave puts us all in his debt, is also now dead. Fortunately Patrick Rogers was able to pick his brains in time. The culmination of many years of study and travel is represented by this wonderful book.

Francis Bartlett used to tell a tale, which is not included here, about William Brindley's search for the Verde Antico quarries which he only identified after sitting down on a rock to rest; his sweaty trousers revealed it to be what he was seeking. Presumably this was one of Mgr Bartlett's stories of the 'ben trovato' variety.

Those of us who show people around the Cathedral will have no excuse for repeating traditional errors, such as the description of the great red granite columns between the narthex and the nave as Norwegian; we learn here that they are Swedish.

Patrick Rogers has already added significantly to the Cathedral bibliography with his numerous articles in *Oremus* (the Westminster Cathedral Magazine), and his book *Westminster Cathedral, From Darkness to Light* (2003). His new book fills a notable gap, and we must all be sincerely grateful to him for doing so in such a scholarly, readable and attractive way.

Peter Howell

(Peter Howell is a former Chairman of the Victorian Society and has been a member of the Cathedral Art and Architecture Committee for more than thirty years.)

INTRODUCTION

It was the intention of J F Bentley, the architect of Westminster Cathedral, to use over 60 varieties of marble to decorate the Cathedral. These were described by his biographer and eldest daughter, Winefride de l'Hôpital, in her book *Westminster Cathedral and its Architect* which appeared in 1919. By this time the number of marbles installed had reached about 50 although Bentley himself had died in 1902. De l'Hôpital's book remains the primary source for the early history of the Cathedral, but of course much of the marble decoration has taken place since then, including the cladding of the nave, narthex, transepts, aisles and many of the chapels. Most of this has been done piecemeal, as money has become available and using the marbles available to marble merchants at the time. As a result well over 100 different varieties have now been employed (129 at the last count), many of them from the same quarries that were used by the Greeks, Romans and Byzantines. This quantity is almost certainly greater than anywhere else in England.

The study starts with a short history of marble, a description of the discovery and exploration of the old quarries, many of which now lie overgrown and abandoned, and an explanation of the sources and methods used in identifying the Cathedral marbles. It continues with a tour of the Cathedral in which the marbles are introduced, followed by a more detailed description of the more interesting of them historically and geologically - those with a story to tell. Part III consists of a series of colour photographs of the Cathedral annotated with the names of the main marbles - a sort of instant guide. The next section, Part IV, lists the marbles to be found in each chapel, transept or other location. Finally, in Part V all the different varieties are brought together in an alphabetical table which gives details of their colour and place of origin, and states where good examples can be found in the Cathedral. The study concludes with explanatory notes (Part VI) and a list of sources (Part VII).

My thanks are due to all those, in England and overseas, who advised in identifying the marbles and helped me to discover the quarries from which they came, particularly marble merchants Gerald Culliford of Gerald Culliford Ltd, Ian Macdonald of McMarmilloyd, Tsalmas Melas of Tsalma Marble, Larissa, Greece, and Ambrose Joyce (father and son) of Connemara Marble Industries, Moycullen, Galway; to Professor Peter Warren of the University of Bristol, Monica Price at Oxford University Natural History Museum, Mike Dorling at the Sedgwick Museum of Geology at Cambridge and Henry Buckley and Dave Smith at the Natural History Museum in London; to Matthew Parkes and Bernadette Mockler of the Geological Survey of Ireland, Dublin, Tom Heldal of the Geological Survey of Norway, Trondheim, and Ian Thomas, Director of the National Stone Centre, Wirksworth, Derbyshire; to Dimitri Diamandopoulos of Ramblers, Catriona Allan of Cnoc a' Chalmain, Isle of Iona, Alfredo Galasso of Rome, Sandra Berresford of Carrara, Nicolas Scarri of Lourdes, Bernadette Scott of Windsor and the late Aelred Bartlett RIP; to Fr Michael Seed sa and to my colleagues on *Oremus* (Westminster Cathedral Magazine), Fr Tim Dean, Blandine Tugendhat, and especially Elizabeth Benjamin and Ron Smail, who brought it all together.

Patrick Rogers

PLAN OF WESTMINSTER CATHEDRAL

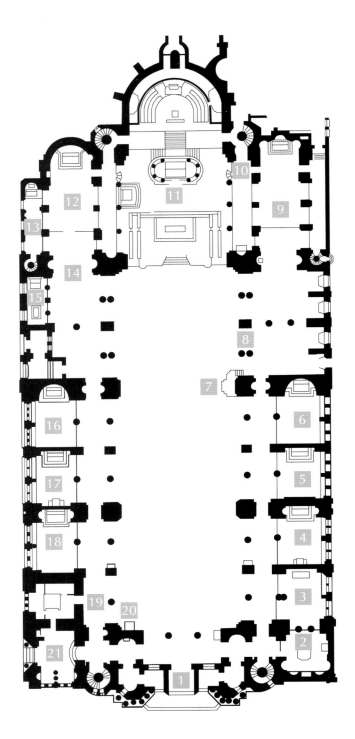

1. Main entrance
2. Baptistry
3. Chapel of St Gregory and St Augustine
4. Chapel of St Patrick
5. Chapel of St Andrew
6. Chapel of St Paul
7. Pulpit
8. Shrine of Our Lady of Westminster
9. Lady Chapel
10. Entrance to crypt
11. High Altar
12. Chapel of the Blessed Sacrament
13. Sacred Heart shrine
14. Peacock and phoenix mosaics
15. Chapel of St Thomas of Canterbury
    (Cardinal Vaughan chantry)
16. Chapel of St Joseph
17. Chapel of St George and the English Martyrs
18. Chapel of the Holy Souls
19. Entrance to the campanile
20. Statue of St Peter
21. Giftshop

Carved marble columns outside St Mark's Venice, seized by the 4th Crusaders from the Church of St Polyeuktos, Constantinople, in 1204.

1. MARBLE IN HISTORY

Egyptian pyramids at Giza, originally encased in polished white limestone of which little now remains.

The word 'marble' comes from the Greek 'marmaros' meaning a white and shining stone and so came to mean an ornamental stone capable of taking a polish. To a geologist marble is a limestone which has been recrystallised (metamorphosed) by great heat and pressure. But to the Greeks and Romans, and most people today, it is simply a fine, hard stone which can be polished and used for architecture, sculpture or decoration. In this study the term will be used in its wider sense and thus will include granites, porphyries and unmetamorphosed limestones.

Methods of quarrying and transporting stone were developed very early on. The world's first stone monument, the Step Pyramid, was built by the architect, Imhotep, at Saqqara in Egypt in 2650 BC. Before that Egyptian temples and tombs were made of perishable materials such as mud-brick. Both the Step Pyramid and later pyramids - notably the three built at Giza about 100-150 years later – were faced with hard, polished white limestone (most of which was subsequently plundered) which was both decorative and protected the softer limestone inside, while the base was protected with red granite. These structures were designed to impress by their sheer size and required huge resources in terms of manpower. The Great

Greek temple of Segesta in Sicily, built about 430BC.

Traces of white stucco on a 5th Century BC Greek Temple at Selinunte, Sicily.

Pyramid at Giza, for example, consists of 2.3 million limestone blocks each weighing 2.5 tons, while a granite obelisk abandoned in the quarry at Aswan is 137 feet long and weighs over 1,000 tons. These great stone blocks were dragged from the quarries on wooden sledges pulled by men and sent on rafts down the Nile to build the pyramids of Saqqara and Giza, the temples of Luxor and Karnak and the tall granite obelisks and statues which we can still see today.

By the 6th century BC the Greeks had adopted Egyptian quarrying techniques such as the cutting of separation trenches and the use of metal or wooden wedges to split the stone away and levers to move it. They also had the great advantage of iron pickaxes, sledgehammers, wedges, mallets and chisels rather than the more primitive stone hammers, wooden mallets, copper and later bronze, points, punches and chisels used by the Egyptians. What the Greek city states lacked was the vast manpower available to Egyptian rulers but they were less concerned with size than with simplicity and harmonious proportions and they had good local building stone readily available. For the most part they used limestone tufa for their temples, which they sometimes coated with white stucco to resemble marble and painted red and blue. But where white marble was locally available of course they used it. Thus in the 5th century BC Pericles, leader of Athens, transformed the Parthenon and other buildings of the Acropolis by the use of hard, white, metamorphic marble from Mount Pentelicon, only 12 miles away.

The most revealing Greek quarries, I believe, are at Cave di Cusa, seven miles west and slightly north of the ancient city of Selinunte (Selinus) in Sicily, which these quarries supplied. They were abruptly abandoned in 409 BC when the Carthaginians attacked and destroyed Selinunte and the quarrymen never returned. As a result the techniques used by the Greeks, such as separation trenches for the men to work in while cutting column blocks, the use of undercutting to detach the blocks from the bedrock, and transport methods, can still be observed. Similar techniques were used by the Romans who, despite their claims to superiority, usually adopted Greek methods.

Generally speaking the Greeks did not favour the use of coloured marble though examples of articles made from Green Porphyry and Rosso Antico have been found dating from Minoan and Mycenaean times. But in the first century BC the Romans

The Glory that was Rome.

became obsessed by it. The Elder Pliny describes critically how six columns of grey Hymettian from near Athens were imported by Lucius Crassus in 95 BC, to be followed by Giallo Antico door sills from North Africa, Africano columns from Asia Minor, Cipollino from Evia in Greece and Carrara from nearby Tuscany. All these marbles, together with white Pentelic, can be found in Westminster Cathedral. It was said that Emperor Augustus found Rome built of brick and left it built of marble. There is a good deal of truth in that and in 17 AD his successor, Tiberius, placed the major quarries under Imperial control. Mass production was introduced, sizes and prices were standardized, the supply chain rationalized and stockpiles built up – as at the Marmorata in Rome and Ostia the local port. Thus a block of Giallo Antico marked as having been quarried in Chemtou in Tunisia under the Imperial slave Felix at the time of the Emperor Domitian (81-96 AD) and stored at Ostia until 394 AD must have been there for about 300 years.

The Romans used slaves and convicts at some quarries and occasionally these became experts. In charge were Imperial officials (slaves or freedmen) and there was often a detachment of soldiers as well. The Romans used essentially the same tools as the Greeks, though their pickaxes were rather heavier. They also used much the same techniques such as separation trenches and the pointillé technique of cutting a series of holes to weaken the rock before splitting it away with a line of wedges. Their teams of draught animals, usually oxen, were generally larger, for the Greeks had marble quarries on their doorstep, whereas the Romans were bringing in marble from far flung quarries in what is now Greece, Turkey, Algeria, Tunisia, Egypt, Spain and the French Pyrenees. Indeed it is remarkable how little the technology and techniques of quarrying and transporting marble changed from the Egyptians until the last years of the 19th century when mechanization and the use of the continuous wire saw, constantly fed with sand and water, was introduced. In some quarries in Italy tradition still reigned until after the 1939-45 War and blocks continued to be wedged out and lowered by hand as in Roman times.

With the fall of the Roman Empire came the so-called Dark Ages and the rule of the Byzantine Empire based in Constantinople. Of course marble was still used, notably by Byzantine Emperors in the 6th and 7th centuries in centres such as Ravenna and Constantinople itself. But its use was much more localized than in Roman times and the main marbles used came from areas relatively close by. Thus Proconnesian came from the Island of Marmara only 70 miles south west of

Constantinople while the Verde Antico used so abundantly in Santa Sophia and other churches in the capital came from quarries in Thessaly, less than 400 miles away across the Aegean Sea. For even under Justinian the Byzantine Empire never controlled the area that Rome had done in its heyday and the Pax Romana no longer held sway on the old Roman trade routes. Generally speaking, where marble was employed (and its use was far from widespread even in churches) local and recycled Roman marble was the rule, up to and including the Middle Ages. In Medieval Italy architects and marble masons turned to the white marble of Carrara, the dark green of Prato, the mottled red and yellow of Verona and the abandoned marble blocks and columns from the old

Carved marble columns outside St Mark's Venice, seized by the 4th Crusaders from the Church of St Polyeuktos, Constantinople, in 1204.

Roman Empire which still lay scattered where they had fallen when the Empire itself fell. In 12th century Sicily the Norman kings used the deep red and white Rosso Antico di Sicilia from Mirto, near Messina, for their new buildings in Palermo and Monreale. For their part the 4th Crusaders, on their way to liberate the Holy Land, were persuaded by Doge Dandolo of Venice (who had promised to provide them with ships) to sack Constantinople in 1204 and loot it of its wealth, including marbles from the Churches of the Holy Apostles and St Polyeuktos which now decorate the Basilica of St Mark's, Venice.

With the Renaissance there came a resurgence of interest in marble. In Florence Cosimo de' Medici, Grand Duke of Tuscany, opened up new quarries across the Apuan Alps and Pisan mountains. In Rome the Church was also engaged in a programme of building and decoration while in France Louis XIV, 'Le Roi Soleil', followed in the footsteps of his ancestors, Francis I and Henry II, and scoured the country for old and new French marbles to decorate his palaces. The Renaissance developed into the age of the Baroque and marble continued to be in vogue. But the French Revolution and the military ambitions of Napoleon resulted in a period of political upheaval in France, Italy and right across Europe, lasting well into the 19th century. It was really only then, with the final defeat of Napoleon and the return of peace to Europe, that things could return to normal and a period of sustained economic growth and prosperity was ushered in. As the century wore on the feeling grew, in national, municipal and commercial circles as well as among private individuals, that wealth meant display, and among the luxury goods in demand was marble.

2. The Marble Seekers

Some of the baldacchino marbles installed by Farmer & Brindley in 1905-6.

It was in Greece that the 19th century marble bandwagon really got under way. After nearly 1,500 years of disuse, in 1834 the old quarries on Mount Pentelicon were reopened to build a palace for the young King Otho of Bavaria. This was followed in 1861 by the extraction of 7,000 tons of Pentelic for the Academy of Science, then more quarrying for the Polytechnic School, the Central Museum, Parliament Buildings and so on as Athens was rebuilt in the neo-classical style. Meanwhile the Greek Government had sent a block of Rosso Antico to London for the Great Exhibition of 1851 and the marble was used for the Albert Chapel at Windsor Castle, for the University Schools building at Oxford and for Byron's memorial statue in London. By the early 1880s the main quarries near Cape Tenaro had been opened up and Greece was exporting the marble in quantity.

It was a French scientific expedition of 1829 to newly independent Greece which first located Rosso Antico, at Paganea in the Mani. They named it 'Marbre Rouge Antique de Skutari'. The French also discovered the old Roman Green Porphyry quarry near Stephania in Laconia. Some twenty-five years later the marble which is today known as Green Tinos was discovered, together with ancient quarries, on the island of Tinos in the Cyclades. Initially this was claimed incorrectly to be the Verde Antico used by the Romans and Byzantines, and marketed as such. Meanwhile the French were intent on developing their own marble industry and from 1835 a thriving export trade began to be built up, mainly to Belgium where French marbles were used for mantelpieces, furniture and clock cases etc. Several French quarries were rediscovered and reopened, notably in 1844 that for Grand Antique des Pyrénées, the striking black-and-white marble which was one of those used for Napoleon's mausoleum at Les Invalides in 1861. For the French Second Empire of 1851-71 was a time when much of Paris was rebuilt and decorative marble was very much in vogue.

It was not only in France that marble was in fashion. The Albert Chapel at Windsor Castle was decorated as a memorial to Prince Albert between 1863 and 1873. It included a series of inlaid marble intarsia pictures by Baron Henri de Triqueti which employed 28 different marbles from Britain and the Continent. Prince Albert's cenotaph and the surrounding walls employed large amounts of French Grand Antique des Pyrénées (always associated with mourning), while the floor consisted of 48 different marbles arranged in a geometric design. The Royal Mausoleum at nearby Frogmore was built in the same period, from 1862-71, and also made full use of marble, including a large block of Emperor's Red from near Lisbon presented to Queen Victoria by Don Pedro, King of Portugal, and Belgian Black (Noir Belge) for the tomb, given by King Leopold of the Belgians. Both the Albert Chapel and the Royal Mausoleum were immensely popular and there were other marble showcases elsewhere. London's Great Exhibition of 1851 proved to be only the first of a series of regular opportunities to advertise rediscovered marbles such as Grand Antique and Campan, to show new uses for them like Triqueti's intarsia technique (exhibited in 1862), and to reveal new machinery for the marble industry like the continuous wire saw which was presented at the Paris Exhibition in 1889.

Of course there were wonderful opportunities for showmen. One such figure was Charles Garnier, chosen from 171 contenders to be the architect of the New Paris Opera House. Work on it started in 1862 and it was opened, amidst great publicity, in 1875. The style he adopted was a new one, 'the style of Napoleon III' as he put it, and the materials he used included many varieties of marble, particularly for the grand staircase. One of these, Swiss Cipollino, was used there for the first time. Twin columns of it are now at the entrance of the Chapel of St Gregory and St Augustine in Westminster Cathedral. Garnier wanted to revive the full-scale use of marble for decoration. But the material was largely available only in small amounts for mantelpieces, paving, tabletops and tombs. So Garnier went looking for quarries which could supply what he needed. The marbles he eventually assembled came from Algeria, France, Italy, Scotland (granite), Sweden and Switzerland. Most, including Grand Antique des Pyrénées and Campan Vert, are also in the Cathedral. Obtaining thirty great load-bearing columns for the grand staircase was a particular problem. After looking at every possibility Garnier chose yellow and red Sarancolin from a quarry halfway up a mountain in the Pyrenees. In January 1863 he went there to inspect the blocks. It was piercingly cold, there was deep snow and the oxen had turned the paths into liquid mud. "C'était horrible" wrote Garnier.

Meanwhile a penniless young Italian from the Del Monte family of marble merchants in Carrara had gone to Algeria soon after the French conquest. His first discovery was of onyx near Tlemçen in 1849. At some risk to his life, for the countryside was still unsubdued, he approached the local Arabs and bought the site for a small sum, subsequently selling it on. Then, in excavations near Arzeu, he discovered mosaics of a totally different marble, so he set out to find its source. What he eventually discovered, in 1874, high on a mountain plateau north-east of Oran, were the marbles of Kleber. French geologists had surveyed the area for iron ore but not for marble; for iron, while not present in commercial quantities, had stained the porous rock red. From a natural creamy white on the eastern plateau the marbles ranged through rose to a red-flushed yellow. To the west, great earth movements had fragmented the rock and water had carried iron oxide into the fissures, staining the breccia from orange to a deep blood-red. Marbles from the quarries, which Del Monte immediately arranged to exploit, now decorate the walls of the Cathedral's Lady Chapel (pink-flushed Giallo Antico), those of the Blessed Sacrament Chapel (deep pink Rose de Numidie), the altar frontal in St George's, the floor in the Holy Souls and the nave piers at gallery level (all Brèche Sanguine).

Back in England events were being closely watched by a young sculptor from Derbyshire, William Brindley. Described by George Gilbert Scott in 1873 as "The best carver I have met with and the one who best understands my needs". Brindley was chosen by Scott for the capitals and other stonecarving on the Albert Memorial. In the 1850s he worked for William Farmer and by 1868 he had formed a partnership with him at 67 (later 63) Westminster Bridge Road. Early commissions, many of them for Scott, consisted mainly of stone and wood carvings for churches but also included plaster models of animals, prior to their execution in terracotta, for the façade of the Natural History Museum in Kensington. But in 1879 William Farmer died and, like Garnier and Del Monte before him, Brindley decided that marble was a material of the future. As he himself put it almost 20 years later "As my delight is in old quarry hunting and as I knew the high price fragments dug up in Rome fetched, I determined to try and find the lost quarries and see if they were worked out or not". Knowing from Garnier's 1878 book about the Opera House that he had failed to obtain Greek Cipollino (he used Swiss instead) Brindley went out to the island of Evia to find it. After previously listing themselves in the Trades Directory simply as sculptors, in 1881 Farmer & Brindley advertised as 'sole Agents for Cipollino'. Columns of this wavy, light green marble are now at the entrance to the Chapels of St Joseph, St Patrick and St Paul and in the Cathedral transepts.

FARMER & BRINDLEY Ltd.

MODELLERS, SCULPTORS, CARVERS & ART WORKERS IN MARBLE, STONE, WOOD, ETC.

The largest Assortment of Marble in the world on view.

The greater part of the Marble Work in the Cathedral (including the Baldacchino) has been executed by this firm.

STUDIO, WORKS, ETC.

63 Westminster Bridge Road, LONDON.

Advertisement by Farmer & Brindley of 1913.

1886 saw Brindley on the Greek island of Chios searching for the ancient quarries of Africano. Instead he found those of Porta Santa, "Pliny was wrong" he complained. The following year, determined to find the source of perhaps the most famous Roman marble, the Imperial Porphyry of the Emperors, he set off into the Egyptian Eastern Desert with nineteen attendants and fifteen camels. After a week in the saddle he found the old Purple Porphyry quarries used at the time of Hadrian on Gebel Dokhan, a mountain twenty-three miles from the Red Sea. By this time, he wrote, "the water from the goatskin tasted like hot, rancid, bacon broth". The following year Farmer & Brindley's listing in the Trades Directory included the words 'Quarry proprietors of ancient Egyptian Porphyry'. Because of the isolation of the desert quarries and the great hardness of the stone, porphyry was not a commercial success, but Brindley's next venture was. Using a description by Paul the Silentiary, Emperor Justinian's court poet, at the opening of the Church of Santa Sophia in 563, Brindley set out to find the source of the celebrated Roman marble, Verde Antico. After a quest which lasted from 1886-94, he found the ancient quarries near Larissa in Thessaly, Greece, and arranged to exploit them. Eight columns of this dark green marble, the first to be hewn for 1,300 years, now line the nave of the Cathedral, with three more at the transepts, while slabs of the lighter variety appear in almost every chapel.

Meanwhile, orders for marble decoration were increasing as Brindley had foreseen. There was a building boom in England from 1897 right through until 1909-10 and marble was fashionable. Major commissions completed by Farmer & Brindley included Surrey House, Norwich (1904), the Victoria and Albert Museum (1909) and the National Gallery (1911). Westminster Cathedral was a continuing source of work. The structural columns with their carved Carrara capitals (1900) were followed by the baldacchino (1906), the Blessed Sacrament Chapel (1907), Lady Chapel (1908), Sacred Heart Shrine, Vaughan Chantry and remaining altars (all 1910), Baptistry floor (1912), St Andrew's Chapel (1915) and St Paul's (1917). Many

The Cathedral pulpit as rebuilt by Fennings of Hammersmith in 1934.

of the marbles used were supplied by the Anglo-Greek Marble Company (Marmor), subsequently known as Grecian Marbles Ltd, formed in 1897 to develop the quarries of Mount Pentelicon and those on the islands of Evia, Paros, Tinos, Skyros and Naxos on systematic lines.

Farmer & Brindley became a private limited joint stock company in 1905 when Brindley, by now 74, effectively handed over to his nephew, Ernest Robert Brindley, and his son-in-law, Henry Wheeler Barnes, and retired to Boscombe in Hampshire. From 1908-23 Farmer & Brindley advertised as 'Largest establishment and with greatest variety and stock of choice coloured marbles and rare stones in the Kingdom'. But the 1914-18 War, coupled with a fall in popularity for the Gothic style with its associated stone and woodcarving, resulted in a gradual decline in the fortunes of the firm. Brindley died in 1919 and without him the heart seemed to go out of the business. London's County Hall and Glasgow's City Council Chambers provided work until 1922-23 but commissions elsewhere were sparse. In Westminster Cathedral the apse wall was decorated in 1921, the organ screen in 1924 and the south transept in 1926, while work on St Patrick's Chapel took place from 1923-29. Here went some of Brindley's rarest remaining marbles - framed panels of Purple Porphyry, dark green Brèche Universelle from Wadi Hammamat in Egypt and lighter green Smaragdite from Corsica for the west wall, with costly Lapis Lazuli and diamonds of grey Africano set in red Languedoc over the niches beside the altar. But without Brindley problems were developing. There was an accident at the works in 1924 and the white marble screen beside the entrance to St Patrick's Chapel was rejected in 1929 and had to be recarved the following year. By this time it was all over for Farmer & Brindley. In 1929 they appeared in the Trades Directory simply as marble decorators. The same year the firm ceased trading. For many years the site on Westminster Bridge Road stood derelict. It is now a block of flats.

Of course it did not all end there. The riverside firm of sculptors and marble merchants, Fenning & Company of Palace Wharf, Rainville Road, Hammersmith (with works at Willow Bank Wharf, Putney Bridge Approach, Fulham), took over from Farmer & Brindley. In 1930 they laid the floor in St George's Chapel, in 1934 they remodelled the old marble pulpit to double its capacity and the following year they started work on St Joseph's Chapel, completing it in 1939 when they laid the floor. During the War Fennings also laid the Cosmatesque floor in the Chapel of St Paul in 1940 and maintained a watching brief, keeping a lorry and six men available at all times to salvage mosaics and marbles should the Cathedral be bombed. After the War, using pre-war stock, the firm resumed the work which they had started in the 1930s on the marble cladding of the nave aisles and the passages either side of the sanctuary, completing this in 1953. Their last significant commission, in 1956, was to lay the marble floor in the Lady Chapel and decorate the nave arcade and gallery balustrade outside the Chapel of St Gregory and St Augustine. But bitter disputes within the Cardinal's advisory art committee over the style and supervision of this project caused problems, not least for Fennings. When money was again available in 1959 to resume the work on the nave, Fenning's estimate of £9,000 per bay was a third higher than that of an equally experienced firm of marble merchants, J Whitehead & Sons.

Advertisement by Whiteheads of 1924.

So Whiteheads got the job. Not that they were newcomers. In 1902 Joseph Whitehead & Sons (Established 1821) of Imperial Works, 64 Kennington Oval had undertaken the decoration of the tribunes and arcades either side of the sanctuary, work described by *The Catholic Herald* in March 1903 as 'A very artistic design which will perhaps be the very best.' Whiteheads were also responsible for the marbles in the Chapel of St Gregory and St Augustine and the Holy Souls Chapel in 1902-06, Cardinal Manning's tomb and the altars to St Edmund and St Paul in 1907-10 and, more recently, the walls of St George's Chapel and marblework in the north transept in 1947-49. But in 1959 the first priority was to obtain the right marbles so Mr Whitehead, together with Aelred Bartlett who was to supervise the project, visited the Greek Cipollino marble quarries on the Island of Evia. There Aelred insisted that marble with wavy, undulating patterns should be obtained which could be 'opened out' to produce the best effect in the Cathedral. He had no water to prove his point on the dusty marble in the quarries but found an alternative. With the help of the Geological Survey of Ireland, Aelred had earlier travelled to Baneshane quarry in Co Cork to find the Cork Red marble last used in the Cathedral in 1928. Meanwhile Francis Bartlett, the Cathedral's Sub-Administrator and Aelred's brother, went out to the Greek Rosso Antico quarries of the Mani and to the hill in Laconia where the Romans extracted Green Porphyry. He later recounted his adventures to an audience at the Brompton Oratory.

On their return to England the Bartlett brothers, working closely with Whiteheads, set about decorating the Cathedral in accordance with the original plans of the Cathedral architect, J F Bentley, using the Greek Cipollino, Cork Red and Rosso Antico they had discovered. The south side of the nave was completed in 1960, the north side in 1963 and the narthex and entrance porches the following year. It is to these men, the artist Aelred and the priest Francis, to the French architect and showman

A craftsman carving Carrara Statuary marble in the 1950s.

Charles Garnier, to the Italian fortune seeker and explorer Giovanni Battista Del Monte, and to William Brindley, the adventurous sculptor and marble merchant, that we owe the appearance of Westminster Cathedral today.

3. IDENTIFYING THE MARBLES

The first step in studying the history and decoration of Westminster Cathedral is to read Winefride de l'Hôpital's *Westminster Cathedral and its Architect*, published in 1919. This lists some 50 marbles - not far short of the number that her father (J F Bentley, the Architect of the Cathedral) planned to use. In Parts IV, V and VI of the present study, which list the Cathedral marbles by location and alphabetically, de l'Hôpital is therefore referred to as Source 1. It is clear from her book that she not only had access to her father's papers - Bentley died in 1902 - but was also provided with information by the Cathedral Clerk of works (C H Mullis) and his assistant (Percy Lamb) together with representatives of the two marble merchants responsible for the early decoration (Henry Barnes of Farmer & Brindley and Joseph Whitehead of J Whitehead & Sons). As a result her identification of the marbles must be regarded as authoritative.

Marble examples at the Sedgwick Museum of Geology, Cambridge.

The next person to study the Cathedral marbles was Francis Bartlett, Sub-Administrator at the Cathedral from 1954-64 and Administrator from 1967-77. In 1954-56 he produced a series of black and white photographs of the Cathedral annotated with the names of the main marbles (Source 3) and in 1989 he published two articles on the marbles in the magazine of the Friends of the Cathedral (Source 2). But he freely admitted, as in a letter to Mary Winearls Porter of 1965, that 'Nothing systematic has ever been done about the Cathedral marbles - when I was there I was always too busy to devote time to it.' Then there are the progress reports on decoration (Source 4) contained in the Cathedral periodicals - particularly the *Westminster Cathedral Record* (1896-1902) and the *Westminster Cathedral Chronicle* (1907-1967) which contain invaluable contemporary information. In the archives there are the architectural plans and drawings of the Cathedral (Source 5), sometimes annotated by Bentley and his successors with the names of marbles. And finally there are those who still remembered what happened - such as Aelred Bartlett (artist brother of Francis) who talked with me deep into the night over Greek olives and Retzina.

A column of Barnanoraun marble in Dublin's Trinity College Museum.

After the Cathedral records the logical next step was to look at other written material on marbles, ideally that written while the Cathedral was being decorated. The main source here is John Watson's *British and Foreign Marbles and other Ornamental Stones* of 1916 (Source 8) as it refers on numerous occasions to the marbles in the Cathedral. Other useful books are those by Blagrove (1888), Renwick (1909), Davies (1939) and Grant (1955). The great advantage of Watson's book is that he describes the extensive collection of marble samples held in the Sedgwick Museum of Geology at Cambridge (Source 14). Thus a colour photograph of an unidentified Cathedral marble can be compared both with Watson's description and with the sample at Cambridge This was also done using some of the thousands of marble samples held by the Natural History Museum in London, at the Oxford University Museum of Natural History where columns of British and Irish marble are on display, and at Dublin's Trinity College Museum and the old Economic Geology Museum at 51 St Stephen's Green where great panels of Irish marble line the foyer.

Identification is much more reliable when columns or large slabs of marble are available for comparison rather than museum samples which are often only six inches square. Being naturally formed, no one piece of marble is completely identical to another. Examples may vary widely in colour and appearance and a single small sample can be misleading. This is another reason why the columns and slabs at Oxford and Dublin are so useful and the books by Watson and Renwick so valuable as these books also give examples of buildings using particular marbles for decoration - as they were intended. Many of these buildings have since gone - the marble-filled Holborn Restaurant in London, for example. But great slabs of Rouge Jaspé, Griotte de Sost and Vert des Alpes, together with columns of Campan Vert, can be studied in the foyer of the Hotel Russell in London's Russell Square; and many other marbles can be found in quantity in particular buildings - the National Gallery, the Victoria and Albert Museum, the Natural History Museum, the Old Bailey, Drapers Hall, the Metropole Hotel (now government offices), the Norwich Union Headquarters in Norwich, Birmingham and Brompton Oratories, etc - and so used for purposes of comparison and identification.

But often a definite match may be more complicated. To give just one example (and there are many more), the paired black and yellow columns in the apse 'balconies' above the choir in the Cathedral had never been identified. A chance visit to County Hall (the old GLC building by the Thames) revealed large columns and pilasters of an apparently identical marble in the, now deserted, Council Chamber. These were on record as Cipollino Dorato marble (also called Veiné Dorée) from a little quarry in Valdieri (Cuneo) in Italy. In 1996 an Italian lady from the area had written to County Hall enclosing photographs of the columns leaving for England in 1925. The opportunity was taken to send photographs of the Cathedral columns to her and she referred these to the Professor of Engineering at the Mining Department of Turin University, a specialist in this particular field. He confirmed that they were indeed Cipollino Dorato from Valdieri.

But written descriptions and photographs can only go so far in identifying marbles and once these are exhausted it is time to turn to marble merchants and other experts. Fortunately Gerald Culliford, Chairman of Gerald Culliford Ltd, and Ian Macdonald, Managing Director of McMarmilloyd Ltd, were willing to help, as was Monica Price, assistant curator at the Oxford University Museum of Natural

Breccia Universale examples in the Michelangelo Collection at the Palazzo dei Conservatori Museum, Rome.

History, and it was as a result of visits to the Cathedral by them that the remaining marbles came to be identified. Just three Cathedral marbles are now outstanding - a black and grey breccia high on the west wall of the narthex (described by Aelred Bartlett as 'that awful Algerian conglomerate'), a dark green, cream and black vertical panel in the aisle outside St George's Chapel (probably an unusual form of Verde Antico) and a light grey marble on the floor below the altar of the Lady Chapel which Winefride de l'Hôpital listed simply as grey Greek marble.

In Parts IV, V and VI of this study the numbers refer to the various sources which were used to identify a particular marble. These sources are listed at the end of Part VII. To avoid misrepresentation, wherever possible the names used by those recording the marbles at the time have been preserved, with explanatory footnotes when necessary. But the study uses information from a variety of sources over the period of more than a century during which time marble quarries have opened and closed and new names have been introduced by marble merchants. Thus although 126 marbles (plus 3 unidentified) from 25 countries on five continents are listed, this number could be increased or reduced depending on the level of differentiation.

PART II

THE MAIN
CATHEDRAL
MARBLES AND
THEIR HISTORY

Ancient Cipollino columns at Kylindroi quarry with Karystos below.

1. A TOUR OF THE MARBLES

An English rose in Rosso Antico marble on the floor of St George's Chapel.

Over a hundred different varieties of marble decorate Westminster Cathedral, almost certainly more than in any other building in England. Many of them were used in ancient Greece, Rome and Constantinople.

On entering the Cathedral by the main entrance you are likely to be standing on light blue-grey Bardiglio Fiorito (floral blue) from the Carrara area of Tuscany. Immediately in front are two red columns, a reminder that the Cathedral is dedicated to the Precious Blood. They are of Swedish* red granite, with bases of dark grey Norwegian Larvikite showing iridescent flecks of silvery mica, and capitals of carved Carrara Statuary marble. All the nave column capitals were meticulously designed by the architect, J F Bentley, in the Byzantine style and each one took two men three months to carve after it had been installed.

Looking down the nave the dark green columns on either side are Verde Antico from Thessaly in Greece. They come from a series of ancient quarries which supplied the columns for Byzantine churches such as Santa Sophia and Sergius and Bacchus in Constantinople, now Istanbul in Turkey. Between the columns are great brick-built piers. The smaller ones are clad with wavy green Greek Cipollino from the Island of Evia (Euboea), used extensively in ancient Rome. The larger ones are faced with Cork Red from near Midleton in Co Cork in Ireland, and light green Campan Vert from the Campan Valley near Lourdes in the French Pyrenees.

Verde Antico and Cipollino columns at the south transept.

Moving to the right down the south aisle we go past the Baptistry and come to the Chapel of St Gregory and St Augustine. Most of the marbles here are Italian - a lovely panel of White Carrara called Acqua Bianca (white water) on the floor above Cardinal Hume's tomb, yellow and black Tuscan breccia below the windows and veined dark red Rosso Levanto from near Genoa for the bench below. The altar frontal is also from Italy, exceptionally beautiful slabs of Yellow Siena, but the great twin entrance columns are waxy Swiss Cipollino from the Canton Valais, while the altar table is Norwegian Pink from Fauske, with the rather attractive title of 'Midnight Sun' - you can see why.

On now to the Chapel of St Patrick where Irish marbles are much employed - wavy green Connemara from the Sky Road near Clifden for the altar frontal and floor, Cork Red for the little columns below the windows, the centre of the altar frontal and also much of the floor, and Kilkenny Black fossil marble for the altar top. But marbles from many other countries also appear. Below the altar is a design combining turquoise Amazon Green from Colorado in America with dark blue Chilean Lapis Lazuli in a surround of green Verdite from Pemberton in the Transvaal of South Africa. Above the niches either side of the altar, French red Languedoc encloses diamonds of red and grey Africano marble - certainly ancient since the old Roman quarry, near Izmir in Turkey, had flooded, become a lake and remained undiscovered until 1966. It started to be called Africano because of its colour, the colour of Africa, and it was one of the first coloured marbles which the Romans used.

Passing between more panels of yellow and black Siena breccia we come to St Andrew's Chapel with its 'pavement like the sea'. Besides being the patron saint of Scotland, St Andrew was a fisherman so the floor uses marble to remind us of this. The central floor panels represent a stormy sea with swirling purple and white Fantastico Viola from Tuscany. The surrounding dark green wave is of Connemara and the light green and white marble, which contains twenty-nine sea creatures, is from the Iona marble quarry in Scotland. This closed at the outset of the 1914-18 War but the workings and abandoned machinery can still be seen. The altar in St Andrew's consists of three Scottish granites - the table of Alloa, the red pillars of Peterhead and the base of Aberdeen.

An English marble can be seen between St Andrew's and St Paul's Chapels. The skirting here is light grey Derbyshire Fossil limestone and contains a myriad of sea creatures which lived and died some 300 million years ago. The grey piscinas either side of the altar in St Paul's are from Wirksworth in Derbyshire - Hopton Wood stone this time. But the main marbles in this chapel are Turkish and Greek. Grey and white banded Proconnesian from the Turkish Island of Marmara lines the wall behind the altar, which is of translucent white Pentelic from Mount Pentelikon near Athens - used to build the Parthenon 2,500 years ago. Dusky grey Hymettian, also from near Athens, lines the walls.

The floor of St Paul's Chapel provides another attraction. Designed by Edward Hutton, it combines Greek Green Porphyry and Verde Antico with Egyptian Purple Porphyry in a nice example of Cosmatesque work. The nearby pulpit, and the delightful floor panel (designed by Aelred Bartlett) below the statue of Our Lady

The Cosmatesque floor of St Paul's Chapel.

of Westminster, are also in the Cosmatesque style. In the 12th and 13th centuries the Cosmati, a Roman school of marble and mosaic workers, cut up and assembled pieces of coloured marble from the ruins of Imperial Rome, and combined them with mosaic tesserae, to produce decorative patterns on floors, pulpits, episcopal thrones, etc. The style is known as Cosmatesque.

Before the Lady Chapel stand two imposing red columns from Languedoc in southern France - so named because the people there said 'Oc' instead of 'Oui', hence Language of Oc. The lower walls in the Chapel display pink flushed yellow Giallo Antico from Kleber in Algeria and dark red Rosso Antico from the Mani in southern Greece. Next door, in the sanctuary, the side columns behind the wooden stalls are also French, Rouge Jaspé from near Toulon, alternating with Norwegian Pink. But the Carrara column capitals remain uncarved. The high altar, twelve tons of Cornish Penryn granite, stands beneath its great canopy, or baldacchino, of white Carrara inlaid with coloured marbles, resting on eight columns of yellow Verona. Looking back down the nave, our 1995 Centenary marbles can be seen fronting the piers high up at gallery level - dark red Rosso Laguna from Turkey** and light blue Azul Macaubas from Brazil.

Another Algerian marble from Kleber, the deeper pink, Rose de Numidie, lines the walls in the Blessed Sacrament Chapel, together with yellow Siena. Further on, the Vaughan Chantry encloses the effigy and tomb of the Cathedral's founder (Cardinal Vaughan) in carved white Pentelic. Two striking black and white columns, known as Grand Antique des Pyrénées or Bianco-e-Nero, stand outside. This French marble from the little village of Aubert in the French Pyrenees was also used in Roman and Byzantine buildings but the quarry is now flooded. Next, to St Joseph's Chapel, where slabs of Cipollino, cut from the same block, have

A central column of Fior di Pesco marble from Tuscany surrounded by other marbles from Italy, Canada and Greece in St Joseph's Chapel.

been opened out or 'book-matched' to create attractive patterns. In front of them below the windows is a central column of Tuscan Fior di Pesco, peach blossom marble, perhaps the most beautiful in the Cathedral.

Next door is the Chapel of St George and the English Martyrs, so many of the marbles are the colour of blood - Greek Rosso Antico inlaid with mother-of-pearl roses on the wall above the altar, Rouge Sanguine from Kleber on the altar frontal, with dark red French Rouge Griotte (called 'Oeil de Perdrix' or partridge-eye because of its pearly white spots or eyes) on the floor, with a red English rose of Rosso Antico in the centre. The final chapel is that of the Holy Souls, with its themes of death and mourning. Here the colours are subdued - an entrance column of silver-grey Norwegian Larvikite surmounted by a mosaic of Adam, facing a column of veined cream Italian Pavonazzo surmounted by a mosaic of Christ - with floor and walls of grey Bardiglio Fiorito and dark swirling green

Verde di Mare (green of the sea) from Genoa. And so we come to the bronze statue of St Peter, the rock on which our Church is founded, and are back to where we started - which is always a good place to stop.

A Pavonazzo column in the Chapel of the Holy Souls.

Listed by Bentley simply as red granite (The Tablet 29.12.1900) but by de l'Hôpital in 1919 as Norwegian, Norway's Geological Survey in Trondheim states that Norway does not (and did not) produce red granite of this type. It appears to be Swedish Imperial Red from Kalmar.

** Not Italian as stated at the time of installation but Turkish from near Becin Kale. Turkish marble is often exported via Italy and described as Italian for commercial reasons.*

2. The Lost Columns

As you enter the Cathedral an avenue of marble columns stretches out before you - first dark green, four on each side, then eight more in pairs as the nave crosses the transepts, and finally eight great yellow columns supporting the baldacchino over the high altar. You would imagine, if you gave it any thought at all, that these columns were selected by the architect, approved by the Cardinal, ordered, quarried, transported, finished and installed as intended. But it didn't happen quite like that - not at all, in fact.

How they should have been. Greek Cipollino and Italian breccia columns at the south transept of the Cathedral.

The eight dark green columns you see first are Verde Antico marble from Thessaly in Greece. The same ancient marble appears throughout Italy, particularly in Rome and Venice, and also in Istanbul (Constantinople) in Turkey. After lying disused for well over a thousand years the quarries were reopened to provide the columns for the Cathedral. The first five marble blocks had been rough-hewn and transported the seven miles to the railhead at Larissa, when Turkey occupied Thessaly in April 1897 and held it until June 1898, preventing shipment for over a year. Thus it was that the Verde Antico columns, on which Cardinal Vaughan had set his heart, were not finally cut, polished and installed until late 1899.

But meantime worse had occurred. When you first look at the eight paired columns where the nave crosses the transepts all seems well. But then you notice that on the left a column of wavy light green Greek Cipollino has been paired first with a column of cream and purple Italian breccia and then with one of Verde Antico - not the lovely dark green Verde Antico of the nave columns but a less attractive variety, possibly from a different quarry. Meanwhile on the right a column of the same Verde Antico stands beside one of Italian breccia while further on breccia and Cipollino are paired. It all looks a bit, well.., cobbled together. Can this be the work of John Francis Bentley, the Cathedral architect, a man renowned for his scrupulous attention to detail?

Well yes it was, but something had happened outside his control. To his dismay, at Farmer & Brindley's marble yards at 63 Westminster Bridge Road across the Thames, three columns, two of them Cipollino and one of Italian breccia, cracked while they were being worked on. To have ordered, quarried, transported, cut and polished replacements from the same quarries would have taken months. After waiting over a year for his Verde Antico nave columns the Cardinal was in no mood for further long delays. The columns were needed at once for the structure of the building. Besides, if Cipollino and Italian breccia were prone to crack could replacements of the same marble be relied on?

What was available, however, were blocks of Verde Antico, released in 1898 from the log-jam caused by Turkish occupation. By 1894 William Brindley of Farmer & Brindley had discovered no less than ten ancient quarries for this marble and in 1896 he had set up the Verde Antico Marble Company to supply it. Verde Antico was a marble particularly liked by the Cardinal and had proved its durability and load-bearing strength over many centuries. It was most unlikely to crack as the other marbles had.

Three of the eight paired transept columns are now of Cipollino and three of Italian breccia. A drawing (F65) by Bentley to show the design of the transept column

The prodigal returned - the Verde Antico column in the aisle to the Blessed Sacrament Chapel.

capitals (of which there are four types), shades all four columns a light Cipollino-like green. This suggests that four transept columns were intended to be of Cipollino and therefore, logically, the remaining four of breccia. It thus confirms that two of the columns which broke were intended for the transepts. So where would they have gone? I believe the present pattern tells us. All three Cipollino columns are on the inner (nave) side, blending in with the Cipollino-clad piers, while all three Italian breccia columns are on the outer (transept) side, reflecting the more varied marbles of the transept walls. This, I believe, was the planned pattern throughout.

But what of the other Cipollino column which cracked and was discarded? There is only one obvious position for it - the aisle leading to the Blessed Sacrament Chapel, a position now occupied by a column of the same light Verde Antico as in the transepts. A Cipollino column here would blend in perfectly with the surrounding Cipollino wall cladding. Indeed there is no other obvious position for it, for Bentley's columns are almost always paired - either side by side or (in the case of chapel entrance columns) across the nave - Languedoc with Languedoc, Swiss Cipollino with Swiss Cipollino, Greek with Greek. An exception is the Holy Souls Chapel where the silver-grey Larvikite entrance column is a fitting prelude for the silver mosaic and grey marble of the interior.

The Verde Antico column in the Blessed Sacrament aisle was also 'lost' for a time - though it subsequently made a comeback. To facilitate processions moving down the aisle, in 1949 the Cathedral authorities had it removed and replaced by a horizontal steel girder. If you look closely at the wall on either side you can see where. The view of the Westminster Cathedral Chronicle that this "will be welcomed by all" was very far from the case. In 1953 the Cathedral Art Committee, which had lapsed, was reinstituted and the column, which fortunately was still in the yard at Fennings of Hammersmith, was restored. It was said that it had been carefully chosen by Bentley. Well ... up to a point.

Finally to the eight columns of yellow Verona marble carrying the baldacchino. Cardinal Vaughan had a contact, Marius Cantini, who owned onyx quarries near Constantine in Algeria and had supplied Marseilles Cathedral. The Cardinal decided on onyx for the baldacchino. In vain was he told that onyx columns greater than five and a half feet had never been produced, he was adamant. At length, in 1902, soon after Bentley's death, the eight onyx columns arrived. Three were already broken and another badly cracked. Two of the others now support the pediment over Our Lady's altar in Birmingham Oratory. The yellow Verona columns originally planned by Bentley were ordered and arrived without mishap in 1905. His baldacchino, on which he had spent so much effort and which he had described as "the best thing about the Cathedral" was unveiled on Christmas Eve 1906.

A hundred and fifty years ago, John Ruskin, that great exponent of the Gothic style, compared the columns of a marble-encrusted building to its jewels. There are a hundred and thirty marble columns in Westminster Cathedral, all of them monoliths, all of them solid, ranging in size from three to fifteen feet. They are its jewels.

Bentley's columns.
The baldacchino
as it is today.

3. Verde Antico

A stele (gravestone) from Roman times now in Larissa museum.

Westminster Cathedral was built in the Byzantine style and among its 100 and more marbles there is one which is truly Byzantine. Verde Antico marble was used extensively in Constantinople, capital of the Byzantine empire, and the ancient quarries which provided it were rediscovered and reopened about 100 years ago to build our Cathedral.

In about 1886 the marble merchant William Brindley visited Constantinople (now Istanbul) and realised that some 75 per cent of the coloured marble in the ancient Byzantine churches there, notably Santa Sofia (the Church of Holy Wisdom), consisted of dark green Verde Antico. This suggested a readily available source for the marble. All knowledge of the quarries had been lost after the Turks had seized Constantinople in 1453 but many centuries before, when Santa Sophia was re-opened by Emperor Justinian in 563, his court poet Paul the Silentiary had described the building and its marbles. To this description Brindley therefore turned.

Verde Antico was described by the poet as 'The marble that the land of Atrax yields, not from some upland glen but from the level plains, in parts fresh green as the sea or emerald stone, or again like blue cornflowers in grass, with here and there a drift of fallen snow a sweet mingled contrast on the dark shining surface'. Elsewhere Paul refers to the Verde Antico columns as Thessalian or from Thessaly - a Greek province 300 miles west of Constantinople across the Aegean Sea. So in the following spring Brindley set off to search for the quarries there, apparently unaware that their location had been previously noted by a Venetian engineer planning the Thessalian railway and that a German geologist (F Teller) had described the quarries in 1880.

Twin Verde Antico columns in the church of Santa Sophia, Constantinople (now Istanbul).

Returning from an unsuccessful search of the site of ancient Atrax in continuous rain, he suddenly noticed what looked like rounded boulders of Verde Antico set into houses in the town of Larissa. An elderly local Turk told him they were gathered in the fields of the plain which lies below the foothills of Mount Ossa. Before returning to England Brindley paid a French road engineer to organise a search for signs of old quarries in these hills. But it was not until after Brindley had sent out sketches he had made of the areas he regarded as most promising, that the first quarry was found, embedded in shale and overlaid with limestone some 300ft above the plain.

The Verde Antico quarries with the quarrymen's church in the distance.

After receiving full particulars by post, Brindley began negotiations through his agent to reopen the quarry. When these were finally completed he returned to Greece, only to find not less than ten ancient quarries producing every shade and variety of the Verde Antico marble to be seen in Constantinople and Rome. They also showed the ancient methods of working, one large quarry face consisting of vertical, almost semicircular, hollows where columns, quite probably for Santa Sophia itself, had been axed around prior to being severed at the base. Elsewhere quarry faces and blocks revealed the marks of saws while one quarry contained a block prepared as a 9ft-long sarcophagus.

The quarries are near Casambala (Hasambali), 7 miles north-east of Larissa on the right of the road to Sikourio. Setting up a company and workforce to clear almost 60ft of rubble and reopen them took two years. In 1896 the Verde Antico Marble Company was established with £20,000 capital at 34 Victoria Street in London and quarrying began. The first five columns to be extracted since the age of Justinian, hand-quarried as in his time, were transported across the plain to the railhead at Larissa towards their final destination in Westminster Cathedral. But then another delay occurred when, in April 1897, Greece attacked Turkey which retaliated by invading Thessaly, capturing Larissa and very nearly the Greek crown prince as well.

Although the war lasted only a week, negotiations over war reparations to Turkey lasted a year. It was not until June 1898 that the Turks finally withdrew, allowing the Verde Antico columns to leave the railway sidings at Larissa and travel down to the port at Volos and from there to Farmer & Brindley's marble works at 63 Westminster Bridge Road, London. There they were turned on a large lathe with steel blades, ground with sand and polished with oxide of tin, finally being put in place in the Cathedral in late 1899 - 13 years after William Brindley had started his quest in 1886.

With Verde Antico again available, demand increased. Blocks measuring thousands of cubic feet were cut direct from the quarry face using a wire saw, and columns were installed in the hall of the Old Bailey and the Norwich Union headquarters (Surrey House), Norwich. The Cathedral received eleven Verde Antico columns, which stand between the nave and the aisles and transepts, though at 13ft they are dwarfed by the 48 great columns of Santa Sophia between 22ft and 25ft 6in in height. Elsewhere in the Cathedral Verde Antico panels can be seen in the nave and organ screen, in the sanctuary and apse and in all but one of the chapels. The marble was last used to decorate the entrance porches in 1963-4 and for Cardinal Heenan's tomb in 1976. The Verde Antico Marble Company was wound up in 1912 but others took over, quarrying by a Greek company (Tsalmas Marmi) continuing until 1985.

Classified as an ophicalcite breccia, from the Greek word 'ophis' meaning snake, Verde Antico is composed of angular pieces of green and black serpentine and white calcite, all cemented together in a lighter green matrix. It is both beautiful and able to bear great weights safely. It was quarried in Thessaly from at least the age of the Emperor Hadrian in the early second century AD to that of Justinian in the sixth. Besides Santa Sophia and other Istanbul churches, such as that of Sergius and Bacchus, there are 24 columns in the nave of St John Lateran in Rome while others contrast with purple porphyry in the façade of St Mark's, Venice. In all there are perhaps 600 columns of the marble in Europe, over 200 in Rome and eleven in the Cathedral - the first to be quarried for more than 1,300 years.

Verde Antico in the Vaughan Chantry of the Cathedral.

4. ROSSO ANTICO

The Cathedral sanctuary screen and steps in Rosso Antico marble.

One of the most prominent of the Cathedral's marbles is Rosso Antico. It can be seen immediately on entering the Cathedral as violet, decorative paving slabs near the entrance and forming the deep red screen and steps which divide the sanctuary from the nave. It has also been used in many of the chapels.

In 1887 the Lambeth marble merchants Farmer & Brindley were advertising Rosso Antico 'from rediscovered quarries of Greece'. They were listed as quarry proprietors of the marble from 1899-1923 and used it for the Cathedral entrance paving in 1903, the sanctuary screen and floor in 1905-6 and the Lady Chapel in 1908. The colour of the marble ranges from purple to violet, sometimes banded with white stripes and black veins. It appears faded when unpolished, scuffed or weathered, as when used on the floor or steps or exposed to the elements. It comes from the Mani, the remote and mountainous central spur of the Greek mainland which reaches out southwards into the Mediterranean Sea.

There are two areas where the marble has been quarried. The first where outcrops of the white banded variety meet the sea at the Kalivia/Paganea promontory, near Skutari in the outer Mani, was rediscovered by a French scientific expedition in 1829. They named it 'Marbre Rouge Antique de Skutari'. Specimens of this marble were sent by Greece to the

Where Rosso Antico meets the sea at Paganea in the Mani.

Great Exhibition in London in 1851, but its use elsewhere seems to have been limited. More recently, quarrying took place at Paganea from about 1949 until 1964 when 20 men with jack-hammers and explosives were employed, and the marbles sent by sea to Piraeus and then to Alexandria and England. The plain, dark red marble used to decorate the transept piers in the Cathedral during this period appears to be from there.

Boulders of Rosso Antico amidst the wild flowers below the heights of Cape Tenaro.

The other area for the marble is in the deep Mani. Outcrops and boulders of Rosso Antico and evidence of small scale quarrying can be seen to the south of the abandoned village of Mianes, on the heights of Cape Tenaro (also known as Cape Matapan), where the Taygetos Mountains finally run into the sea, and below at sea-level near Porto Kisternes and Kanoghia. The pedestal for a statue of Lord Byron, presented by the Greek Government and erected at Hyde Park Corner in 1881, was reported in *The Times* to 'be the Rosso Antico of the quarries at Cape Matapan'. An earlier memorial statue of Byron by Thorwaldsen had been refused admission to Westminster Abbey by Dean Ireland because of his lifestyle and went to Trinity College, Cambridge. Rosso Antico panels were also used on the floor of the Oxford Examination Schools building, completed in 1882.

The main quarry face at Profitis Ilias with a sheer drop below.

But it is 7 miles further north, close to the deserted village of Profitis Ilias (Elias) and 2 miles west of the local harbour at Aghios Kiprianos (where Marmor had its local base), that several quarries, some ancient, can be found and the hilltops and the village itself stand above mounds of purple marble rubble resulting from early 20th century quarrying. The ancient quarries were discovered in 1850 by a sculptor and lecturer at the Athens Polytechnic School named Siegel, and by 1902 it was reported that the firm of Marmor, based at 18 Finsbury Square in London and the largest quarry owners in Europe, had purchased the site and was opening up the quarries to extract the regularly banded, red and grey Rosso Antico marble to be found there.

But of course Rosso Antico was used long before the 19th century. Indeed the term 'antico' indicates its use in Classical times. Carved blocks decorated the Treasury of Atreus in 13th century BC Mycenae and can be seen in the British Museum. But it was during the Roman Empire, particularly under Hadrian in the second century AD, that Rosso Antico was most popular, both for buildings and for sculpture - notably a bust of a priest and several statues of fauns (companions of Bacchus, the god of wine). Much Roman Rosso Antico was later reused, as in the sanctuary steps of the church of Santa Prassede in Rome.

The stone continues to be used in the Mani. It can be seen set into churches, private houses and even garden walls. But overgrown tracks and long abandoned quarries show that overseas demand has moved on. It seems not inappropriate that here in the Cathedral this ancient purple marble, associated with ritual and red wine, should decorate the entrance to the sanctuary, where Mass is celebrated.

5. Cipollino

Marbles and onions are not usually associated, but the Italian for onion is 'cipolla' and Cipollino marble received its name because of its resemblance to a cut onion. Greek Cipollino is believed to have been one of the first coloured marbles brought to Rome and it was the one most used. In Westminster Cathedral it can be seen cladding walls and piers in the nave, lining the wall of the apse and in virtually every chapel.

Cipollino outcrops on the slopes of Mount Ochi, Evia.

Cipollino has become a term for marble banded with different shades of green, white and yellow. Thus besides Greek Cipollino, the Cathedral also has columns of the waxy yellow Swiss Cipollino (from Saillon in the Canton Valais) at the entrance to St Gregory's, St Andrew's and St George's Chapels. The green veined but more putty coloured Italian Cipollino alternates with the darker Connemara Green marble behind the altar on the wall of St Patrick's and can also be found in St Paul's Chapel. But these have been used for perhaps 200 years whereas that from Greece has been used for over 2,000.

Greek Cipollino was worked first by the Greeks and then by the Romans. Pieces for mosaic floors were brought to Rome as early as the second century BC. But it was in Julius Caesar's time, about 48 BC, that solid columns and wall panels from Carystus were first recorded as being used for a private house. Carystus (Karystos) is on the south-west coast of the Greek island of Evia (Euboea) and the Romans named the marble Marmor Carystium. The quarries were worked extensively as Imperial property until Byzantine times, the 'fresh green of Carystus' being used in Justinian's Church of Santa Sophia in Constantinople, reopened in 563.

Today Cipollino can be found throughout the old Roman Empire. There are over 500 columns in Rome itself. The Temple of Antoninus and Faustina in the Roman Forum has ten columns of the marble 38ft in height. Slabs can be seen on shop counters in Pompeii and Herculaneum and all across Italy and Greece, as well as in Roman outposts such as Carthage. Recycled Cipollino can also be found in many Christian churches. There are eight columns of it in the portico of St Peter's in Rome, and St Mark's in Venice has smaller columns beside one of the entrances with slabs of it on the interior walls and floor.

Five ancient Cipollino columns at Kylindroi quarry with Karystos below.

For 1,300 years the old quarries lay forgotten. But in the 1860s Charles Garnier wrote to Greece for Cipollino for the new Grand Opera House of Paris (opened in 1875). He was told that the quarries were abandoned and the cost would be prohibitive. So Garnier was the first to use the recently discovered Swiss Cipollino

An ancient Cipollino column still attached to the rock in the quarry on Mount Ochi.

instead. He described the incident in his book on the Opera House in 1878 and it appears to have been this which motivated the marble merchant William Brindley to travel to Evia to search out and reopen the ancient quarries there.

Brindley's search lasted several years. It culminated in the discovery of workable marble in a series of old Roman quarries on the side of Mount Pyrgadi, near Styra. These quarries Brindley subsequently exploited. Some 13 miles to the south-east and 3 miles north-east of Karystos, he found Kylindroi quarry where ten ancient columns still lie halfway up Mount Ochi (Ocha). One of these remains attached to the parent rock and another, 38ft in length, is the same size as those in the Temple of Antoninus and Faustina in Rome. In 1881 the Post Office Directory entry for Brindley's firm, Farmer & Brindley, included the words 'Sole agents for Cipollino'. The 1885 entry read 'Sole agents for rediscovered Roman quarries, Numidian, Cipollino, Pavonazzetto'. Two years later Brindley told the Royal Institute of British Architects that 'Good Cipollino is now again obtainable'.

How much Cipollino was supplied by Farmer & Brindley is unclear. They were listed as agents for the marble until 1899 when this changed to 'Quarry proprietors of Egyptian Porphyry, antique Greek Cipollino and Rosso Antico'. But two years earlier, in 1897, the Anglo-Greek Marble Company (Marmor), the largest in Europe with capital of £350,000, had been formed to develop quarries at Pentelikon, Paros, Tinos, Skyros, Naxos and Evia. By 1909 Marmor was advertising as sole suppliers of Cipollino 'from the original ancient Greek quarries'. Farmer & Brindley became a private limited joint stock company in 1905, when Brindley effectively retired at the age of 74, and any active new quarrying ventures by the firm seem to have ended.

The first recorded consignment of Cipollino from Evia reaching London was in 1898. It was of slabs for the new staircase walls at Drapers' Hall and four columns for the Royal Academy of Arts. Shortly afterwards eight more columns arrived for Westminster Cathedral. The marble merchants were Farmer & Brindley. Two of the columns for the Cathedral cracked while being worked but the remaining six can be seen at the transepts and at the entrance to St Patrick's, St Paul's and St Joseph's Chapels. Imports continued. Norwich Union's 1904 headquarters in Norwich received 16 Cipollino columns and eight more went to decorate the 1907 Old Bailey entrance hall. By that time, according to Brindley, over 100 large columns had been produced for Britain, Germany and the USA.

Cipollino produces sound, load-bearing, monolithic columns, as can be seen in the Cathedral. But it also has another quality. Consecutive slabs from a block can he opened out or 'book-matched' to form a continuous and attractive pattern. Cipollino used in this way can be seen in both Santa Sophia in Istanbul and in St Mark's, Venice, but the wealth of Cipollino in the Cathedral has produced probably the best examples of this technique in Britain. These can be seen all around the Cathedral, as on the piers of the nave, in the transepts and bridges above them and on the walls of St Joseph's Chapel.

In early 1956 it was decided that the nave should be clad with marble, including Cipollino, in accordance with the original plans of the Cathedral architect, J F Bentley. Farmer & Brindley were no more and it was Mr Whitehead of J Whitehead & Sons, accompanied by Aelred Bartlett, brother of Francis, the future Cathedral Administrator, who went to Evia to choose the marble. Whiteheads were satisfied with readily available Cipollino with straight, parallel lines. But Aelred wanted the (more expensive) marble with irregular waves and undulating patterns for opening out, and he insisted on the start of a new quarry face to achieve this. The attractive patterns provided by the Cipollino in the nave of our Cathedral today are the result.

*Book-matched Cipollino
in the south transept
of the Cathedral.*

6. White Pentelic

Unlike the Romans, the Greeks were unimpressed by coloured marble. What they wanted for their temples was pure white marble, which they often then painted. They found it on Mount Pentelicon, close to Athens, and Pericles used it for the Parthenon and other great Athenian monuments in the 5th century BC. In the Cathedral it appears in the entrance porches and forms the column bases and canopy above the altar in St Andrew's Chapel, but it can be seen most effectively in the carved effigy of Cardinal Vaughan, the Cathedral's founder, in the Vaughan Chantry.

Of course many Greek temples were not made of marble but of sandstone, limestone or volcanic tufa, which the Greeks covered with white stucco to resemble marble. But Athens was fortunate in having a source of pure white,

The effigy of Cardinal Vaughan carved from White Pentelic marble.

metamorphic marble on Mount Pentelicon, twelve miles to the north-east. All the earlier temples on the Acropolis had been destroyed by the Persians in 480 BC so Pericles, then leader of Athens, set about turning it into a city of temples built of white Pentelic marble. The blocks were detached with iron wedges, sledge-hammers and levers, then hauled up from the quarry on wooden sledges and oak rollers and down to the loading platform from where they were pulled on wagons by teams of mules or oxen to the Acropolis construction site.

In this way the Athenians built the Parthenon to house the great statue of Athena (guardian of Athens) from 447-438 BC, the Propylaia (ceremonial entrance to the Acropolis) from 437-432, the Temple of Athena Nike from 427-424 and finally the Erechtheion (sanctuary) from 421-406. The quarry which provided the marble for these buildings is the oldest on Mount Pentelicon and is known as Spelia (cave). It is estimated that during the summer months at least fifteen wagons a day must have travelled back and forth between the loading bay below the quarry and the new buildings arising on the Acropolis. Spelia Quarry continued to operate on a declining scale for several centuries after this, the zenith of Classical Greek architecture.

The Romans also used white Pentelic, examples in Athens being the Arch of Hadrian and the Temple of Olympian Zeus (which they completed). Although they had their own local white statuary marble quarries at Carrara in Tuscany, they also imported Pentelic marble into Rome from the 1st century BC to the 4th century AD. It was used there,

The Erechtheion (left) and the Parthenon in Athens.

Repairing old column blocks with new Pentelic marble at the Parthenon.

inter alia, for the forum of Augustus, the Arch of Titus and the column capitals for the porch of the Pantheon. After Rome fell there was little demand for the marble and, from the 6th to the 16th centuries, Spelia quarry became the site of small Christian churches and hermitages where asceticism flourished, as well as a place of refuge from pirates. From the mid-17th century until the 1960s it also provided a tourist attraction for Athenians and foreign travellers.

Modern exploitation of Pentelic marble began slowly in 1834, after almost 1,500 years of disuse and in 1836, by royal decree, quarrying began again at Spelia Quarry for marble to build a palace for King Otho of Athens. Then came the Academy of Science in 1861, the Polytechnic, the Central Museum and the buildings of Parliament. Although blasting took place near the ancient quarries and new roads were built, initially little damage was caused. But in 1897 the Anglo-Greek Marble company (Marmor) was formed and the marble exported on a large scale to Britain, other European countries and the USA, for buildings such as Mappin and Webb and D H Evans in Oxford Street, plus, of course, Westminster Cathedral.

After the surge in demand for the marble in the early 1900s, war and recession curtailed activity. Since then, over the last fifty years, post-war reconstruction and the demand for neo-classical buildings in Athens have resulted in unrestrained, sometimes illegal, quarrying on Mount Pentelicon. This has been exacerbated by excavation and blasting for military works from 1976-88, causing the foundations of Spelia Quarry to collapse. Sadly, about 90% of the ancient workings have been destroyed and there is little now to be seen.

Mount Pentelicon - scarred with modern quarries.

Even the old peaceful mule path, fringed with pine trees and used to carry the marble to the Parthenon 2,500 years ago, is now blocked with great mounds of unstable and hazardous marble rubble from recent quarrying activities, together with the occasional empty diesel oil barrel.

7. Green Porphyry

The ruined watch tower on the Hill of Psephi, with a weathered block of Green Porphyry in the foreground.

'As you go down to the sea towards Gythium you come to a village called Croceae and a quarry. It is not a continuous stretch of rock, but the stones they dig out are shaped like those from a river; they are hard to work, but when worked sanctuaries of the gods might be adorned with them'.

Thus wrote Pausanias in his travel guide to Greece of the 2nd century AD. The stone he was describing was Green Porphyry, Lapis Lacedaemonius to the Romans. It is an igneous (volcanic) rock consisting of olive-green felspar speckled with lighter green crystals of the same material - polygonal, cross or star-shaped. The Romans opened the quarry under Emperor Augustus, about the time of the birth of Christ, and the marble from there, together with Purple Porphyry from Egypt, was later listed as the most expensive in Rome (Diocletian's Edict of Maximum Prices of 301 AD) being priced at 250 denarii (£25) a cubic foot. But long before the Romans, the Greeks were using it to contain libations to the gods, as shown by the recovery of a spouted bowl and a vase-shaped rhyton from 14th century BC Mycenae, and unworked blocks of the marble from a workshop in Knossos, Crete.

Boulders of the marble can be seen today emerging from the soil between the villages of Alai Bey (now Faros) and Stephania in Laconia, beside the road from ancient Croceae to the sea north-east of Gythion. The main quarry was on a hill named Psephi, which overlooks the road about half-way between the two villages. On the summit stands a ruined Turkish watch-tower with views across the plain towards the distant sea. The tower, said locally to have been destroyed by the Americans during the Second World War, is concealed from the road by olive trees and is itself overgrown by bushes and wild flowers. Around it, and on the southern and western slopes below, lie boulders and fragments of Green Porphyry, many of them now a speckled rusty brown colour as a result of centuries of exposure to the elements.

A broken boulder of Green Porphyry on the Hill of Psephi.

Because blocks of more than a few feet in size were rare, the Romans used the marble almost entirely in small pieces, often in combination with Purple Porphyry, to produce colourful Opus Alexandrinum or Opus Sectile patterns for inlaid pavements, baths and fountains. It was subsequently widely used by the Byzantines - in the churches of Santa Sophia in Istanbul and San Vitale in Ravenna, for example - and was recycled by the Cosmati marble workers in Rome in the 12th and 13th centuries, again often in combination with Purple Porphyry, to produce decorated floors, pulpits, bishop's thrones etc. But the marble used at this time had previously been used by the Romans, for the ancient quarry in Greece was not rediscovered until 1829 when a French scientific expedition came across it, and it has never been reopened for commercial purposes.

In Westminster Cathedral panels of Green Porphyry, paired with the Egyptian purple variety, can be seen decorating the pulpit, made in Rome in 1902 though remodelled in 1934. It was also used on the floor of St Joseph's Chapel in 1939 and, rather more successfully, on that of St Paul's in 1940. This floor, like the pulpit, is in the style of the Cosmati. The marble merchants responsible, Fennings of Hammersmith, had great difficulty obtaining the Green and Purple Porphyry traditionally used in such floors, and were often forced to employ several different pieces to make up one roundel. They also resorted to extensive use of the more readily available Verde Antico marble. The last time the

Green Porphyry on the floor of St Paul's Chapel in the Cathedral.

marble was used in the Cathedral was in 1960, for inlaid paving (also Cosmatesque) below the statue of Our Lady at the 13th Station of the Cross. But the largest example, of unknown date, is an irregularly shaped block supporting a crucifix, on the staircase above the main entrance to Clergy House.

8. Purple Porphyry

Purple Porphyry, also called Imperial Porphyry, is the most valuable of all the Cathedral's marbles. Known to the Romans as Lapis Porphyrites and to the Byzantines as the Stone of Rome, the quarries were Imperial property and the porphyry itself initially reserved for the Roman emperors. When it finally became available for purchase and a price was put on it by the Emperor Diocletian in 301 AD, it was valued at 250 denarii a cubic foot - the highest price for all marbles.

The name porphyry is derived from the Latin 'purpureus', meaning purple, the Imperial colour. It is dark purplish red spotted with white crystals and is an ignimbrite, molten magma formed at very high temperatures in the

Gebel Dokhan - the Mountain of Smoke - in the Egyptian Eastern Desert.

earth's interior in the Pre-Cambrian period - about 600 million years ago or more - which has cooled and solidified below the surface. The quarries are situated some 4,000ft up a mountain, Gebel Dokhan, the Mountain of Smoke, in Egypt's Eastern Desert. An unpaved Roman road linked them to Keneh, 96 miles to the south-west on a bend of the Nile near Thebes, and to the Red Sea port of Myos Hormos (Mouse Harbour), 23 miles to the north-east.

The fort at the center of the quarry complex with the quarries behind.

To these quarries at Gebel Dokhan, Mons Porphyrites to the Romans, were sent stonemasons, Imperial civil servants and support staff protected by soldiers. Contemporary sources indicate that Christians and other convicts were also sent to work at the quarries though no proof of this has yet been found at the site. At the quarry face porphyry blocks were split away along a line of deep incisions (cut by chisel), by inserting metal or wooden wedges, the latter then being soaked with water to make them swell. The blocks were then shaped with chisels and lowered down the steep mountain ravines, probably on wooden sledges tethered by ropes to stone cairns placed on either side. Once on level ground the porphyry blocks were loaded from ramps onto wagons to be pulled the 100 miles or so down to the Nile and from there by water to Alexandria and thence to Rome.

Purply Porphyry columns decorating St Mark's, Venice.

The settlement has not been fully excavated but coins, inscriptions and written records indicate that the quarries were worked at least as early as the first century AD, one inscription in a shrine being discovered from the reign of the Emperor Tiberius in 18 AD. But increasing external pressure on the boundaries of the Roman Empire finally led to the settlement being abandoned at some stage in the 4th century after the time of Constantine the Great (306-337 AD), all the signs being that the exodus was abrupt and hurried.

For 1,400 years Mons Porphyrites was known only to the Bedouin. It was rediscovered by the British explorers James Burton and Sir Gardner Wilkinson in 1822-23. Wilkinson made detailed notes and plans and sent back samples of porphyry to England. Others followed and in 1887, William Brindley, co-founder of the firm which was later to undertake most of the marblework in Westminster Cathedral, also set off for the quarries. Leaving Keneh with his wife, nineteen attendants and fifteen camels, he reached the mountain in six days and, following old Roman tracks, climbed up to the quarries where he found porphyry of every description and variety, some partly wedged from the face. On returning to Keneh and then to Cairo, Brindley negotiated a concession to rework the quarries.

In 1888 the London Trades Directory entry for the firm of Farmer & Brindley included 'Quarry proprietors of ancient Egyptian Porphyry'. Brindley planned to use Myos Hormos, less than 25 miles away, to send the porphyry through the Suez Canal to England. But the combination of the great hardness of the rock and its location, the absence of sufficient water and the availability of only rock-strewn and partly washed away Roman roads and the need to carry heavy loads over soft sand, proved insurmountable. By 1907 the quarries had still not been worked and Brindley was calling on others to take on the challenge. A few blocks were used for public buildings in Cairo in the 1930s and in 1989 an English sculptor, Stephen Cox, travelled to Gebel Dokhan to obtain porphyry for the new Cairo Opera House. Cox continued to work in Egypt and produced several more works in porphyry including the altar, font, consecration crosses and Stations of the Cross for St Paul's Church, Harringay, in 1993. Since then boulders of Purple Porphyry from the valley below the quarries have been supplied at the rate of about 150 cubic metres a year by an Egyptian firm, Field Investments Egypt, but the old Roman quarries remain untouched as archaeological sites.

In the first century AD the elder Pliny wrote that the porphyry quarries of Egypt could furnish blocks of any dimension, however large. The Emperor Constantine's column in Constantinople (still standing though much damaged) was 100ft high, made up of nine cylindrical drums each 11ft in height and diameter. Two centuries later, eight columns almost 40ft high were used to decorate the Church of Santa

Sophia, Constantinople, sent to the Emperor Justinian from Valerian's Temple of the Sun in Rome. Smaller columns decorate the façade of St Mark's, Venice with more porphyry used for the pulpits. There are some three hundred porphyry columns in Europe (mainly in Rome), numerous sarcophagi and innumerable slabs, including a circular one 8ft 6in across on the floor of St Peter's, Rome - traditionally where Holy Roman Emperors from the time of Charlemagne were crowned.

In the 12th and 13th centuries, the Cosmati school of craftsmen in marble and mosaic, taking their inspiration from the Arab-Norman-Byzantine style to be seen in Sicily, revived the ancient art of Opus Sectile in Rome by cutting up old marble to form patterns on church floors and furniture. The designs centred on roundels, usually of porphyry, and the practice was widely copied. Original Cosmati work can be seen on the sanctuary floor in Westminster Abbey. In Westminster Cathedral the pulpit (originally made in Rome) and the floor of St Paul's Chapel are decorated with porphyry roundels, panels and chips in the Cosmatesque manner. The altar in St Paul's and the floor of St Joseph's are also inset with porphyry while panels decorate the east and west walls of St Patrick's and the east wall of St Andrew's. According to the *Westminster Cathedral Chronicle* of September 1928, just after the west wall of St Patrick's had been decorated, the two panels of Purple Porphyry there were cut from a block brought to England by Lord Elgin and credibly reputed to have come from the Temple of Diana (Artemis) at Ephesus. If so, they could well have witnessed the riot caused by the activities of St Paul in that city (Acts 19). A single slim porphyry column is used as a lectern in the crypt of the Cathedral.

Purple Porphyry on the floor of St Paul's Chapel in the Cathedral.

9. Carrara

When marble is mentioned many people will think of the structures of ancient Rome. Others may remember the buildings and sculptures of the Renaissance, London's Marble Arch or churchyard monuments. Most of these originated in the Carrara region of Italy, the world's largest producer of white marble. But the area produces around sixty varieties of marble, some coloured, and many of them can be found in Westminster Cathedral.

White Carrara marble in the Fantiscritti valley.

Carrara lies between the mountains and the sea in north-west Tuscany. The main quarries are in the Colonnata, Fantiscritti and Ravaccione valleys but the marble mountains of the Apuan Alps stretch 20 miles from Carrara in the west to the villages of Seravezza and Stazzema to the east. The marble was formed some 200 million years ago from the remains of marine creatures accumulating on the seabed. Gradually these became exceptionally pure limestone. About 50 million years ago the European and African continental shelves collided and forced the region downwards. The immense heat and pressure recrystallised (metamorphosed) the limestone into shining white marble which was later forced upwards again to form the Apuan Alps.

In England the white marbles of Carrara have traditionally been divided into Sicilian, Vein and Statuary. It is still not clear why the name 'Sicilian' was used in England and nowhere else. Napoleonic Europe was under British naval blockade in the early 19th century. Indeed Napoleon made his sister, Elisa, Princess of Lucca, only 30 miles from Carrara itself. But Sicily was outside Napoleon's control and was being used by the British. To call marble from Carrara 'Sicilian' is just the sort of cocking a snook at the authorities and private joke that marble merchants (then and now) would have enjoyed. Anyway, that's my theory. Sicilian, or White Carrara (Bianco Carrara) is extremely hardwearing and is the only pure white marble which can be used outside, so it was used for Marble Arch, the Albert Memorial and numerous municipal and graveyard monuments and gravestones. The other types are softer and deteriorate in the open air. In Vein marble (Bianco Venato) the markings are more accentuated. It is generally used for the decoration of the interior of buildings and includes varieties like Arabescato made up of white polygonal shapes divided by grey veining. Statuary (Statuario) is softer still and easy to carve but liable to staining and decay as a result of environmental pollution. Second Statuary or Vein Statuary also contains some veining but is hard enough to be used for paving.

A quarry on Monte Altissimo - Michelangelo's mountain.

The superstructure of the baldacchino in the Cathedral sanctuary employs carved Carrara Statuary marble.

Fine-grained Statuary marble (suitable for sculpture) is found in stratified beds all along this mountain range. In Westminster Cathedral it was used for the column capitals, each one of which took two stonemasons from Farmer & Brindley three months to carve, using chisels and hand-drills in situ. More recently a variety of Carrara marble called Acqua Bianca (white water) was used for Cardinal Hume's tomb in the Chapel of St Gregory and St Augustine. Most marble from the Carrara region is not, in fact, pure white. Veining and shading result from the presence of mineral deposits during formation. Lightly veined Second Statuary was used for the marble floor of the Cathedral while the more heavily veined Arabescato is on the walls and floor of St George's Chapel. Below the stratified beds of white and white vein marble in the mountains, lie beds of a generally blue-grey colour. The darker grey were known in England as 'Doves' and examples can be seen at the corners of the Chapel of the Holy Souls. Lighter blue-grey marble, traversed by darker veins, is Bardiglio Fiorito. It paves the narthex floor and is on the walls and floor in the Holy Souls.

Great earth movements millions of years ago also resulted in fragmentation of the marble, allowing water-borne minerals to penetrate and stain it a variety of colours before it gradually resolidified. Thus the breccias were formed. Columns of Breccia di Seravezza front the organ loft above the narthex and are paired with green Verde Antico and Cipollino columns at the transepts. Breccia Violetta, of a more pronounced violet hue and also from Seravezza, can be seen on the walls of the entrance lobbies and set into the baldacchino. Finally, as if to demonstrate the variety of marbles from the Seravezza area, a column of Fior di Pesco (peach blossom) marble stands against the wall in St Joseph's Chapel, while one of blue Bardilla (or Bardiglietto) stands opposite in St Paul's.

The ancient Etruscan-Roman port of Luni or Luna, about five miles west of modern Carrara, was founded in 177 BC and was the centre of the local marble industry in Roman times. Luna marble was in large-scale use in Rome by 36 BC and about ten years earlier, Mamurra, who lived on the Coelian Hill, was the first to have only solid marble columns in his whole house, these being of Carystus (Greek Cipollino) or Luna marble. Mamurra was Julius Caesar's prefect of works and probably organised the exploitation of the quarries for his building programme. Subsequently Emperor Augustus used the marble extensively for temples and other buildings in Rome. For the next 150 years Luna supplied most of Rome's white marble, examples of its use being Trajan's Column and that of Marcus Aurelius, both well over 100 feet high. From the late 2nd century AD onwards, however, more costly and fashionable marbles from overseas, notably Proconnesian and Pentelic, came to predominate.

For a thousand years the Carrara quarries were largely deserted until again being extensively used in the Renaissance. Duke Cosimo de' Medici in Florence was anxious to exploit the mineral wealth of Tuscany and Michelangelo claimed to have introduced the art of quarrying to Carrara. He became a well-known figure in his goatskin boots as he tramped the hills and valleys of the region and tales are still told of his exploits. There he found the marble for the sculptures which made his reputation - the Pietà now in St Peter's, Rome, which he created when only 24 and which was the only work which he ever signed, the David which symbolised the Florentine Republic, and the figure of Moses intended for the tomb of Pope Julius II and in the beard of which (so it is said) are carved portraits of both the Pope and Michelangelo himself. But to his dismay the new Pope, Leo X, sent him to the unexploited Monte Altissimo region above Seravezza for marble for the façade of

All five columns together with capitals and bases, in St Paul's Chapel, are from the Carrara area.

the Medici church of San Lorenzo in Florence. In the event San Lorenzo remained unclad brickwork but marble from the region was used for both the Duomo in Florence and St Peter's Basilica in Rome.

There are 200-300 active marble quarries in the Carrara region, less than half the number of a century ago. But mechanisation has resulted in around a million tons of marble being produced annually, mostly for the Middle East, and great blocks can be seen at the quarries inscribed 'Egypt', 'Libya', or 'Syria'. Until the end of the 19th century the marble was quarried with pickaxes, chisels and wedges and allowed to slide down the mountains on wooden sledges before being carried away by bullock wagon - practices unchanged since Roman times. Only in 1898 was the endless wire saw, constantly fed with sand and water and used in conjunction with the penetrating pulley, introduced into the quarries. Meanwhile in the town of Carrara, the main processing centre, marble blocks are now sawn into slabs for walls and floors using diamond bladed saws, and full-size marble statues are created from the plaster models of sculptors.

10. Portoro

Unlike many of the Cathedral marbles, which were used by the Greeks, Romans and Byzantines, Portoro or 'black and gold' marble is a product of the Italian Renaissance, being first used by the Medici in 16th century Florence.

The view from the Portoro quarries of the Church of San Pietro, Portovenere, with the sea behind.

Portoro or Portor is a corruption of the Italian 'Porto d'Oro' or 'Port d'Oro'. It was formed in the Triassic period, about 200 million years ago, and consists of black low-grade metamorphosed limestone traversed by golden yellow veins of feruginous clay. It can be divided into 'Portoro a Macchia Fine' with narrow veins and patches, and 'Portoro a Macchia Larga' with broad yellow veins and patches, which stand out against the dark background. Early quarries lie alongside a long distance footpath (the Sentiero Rosso) on the hillside above the ancient harbour town of Portovenere, at the entrance to the Gulf of La Spezia in Liguria, just over the border from Tuscany. The marble was also quarried on a nearby island, the Isola della Palmaria, and quarrying still continues in the region, known as the Cinque Terre. But the Second World War and its aftermath disrupted trade and the old quarries now lie abandoned together with engines and marble cutting machinery which appear to have been made in the late 19th and early 20th centuries.

The marble was originally located and exploited in the mid 16th century under Cosimo I, Grand Duke of Tuscany and patron of the arts, being used to decorate walls, floors and other architectural features in Florence and elsewhere. In France too, Portoro was used extensively as inlay for Boulle furniture, its golden yellow veins set against a deep black background blending perfectly with gilded wood. As a result Portoro continued to be used in France for furniture, fireplaces, clock-cases and other decorative features right up until the Revolution and subsequently under the Empire. In the 19th century it was employed in Paris for the lavish decoration of the Church of La Madeleine (consecrated 1842) and again returned to favour in the 20th century during the Art Nouveau period.

In Westminster Cathedral it was one of the first marbles to be used, by the marble merchants Whiteheads for the altar frontal of the Chapel of the Holy Souls in 1902. It was also employed for the skirting of this chapel though what we see now is a replacement, installed by the firm of Farmer & Brindley in 1927. Whiteheads also used it for skirting in the Chapel of St Gregory and St Augustine and the Baptistry screen, also in 1902.

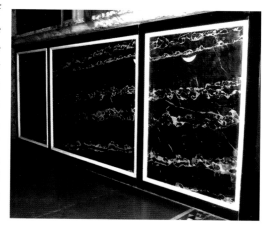

Three panels of black and yellow Portoro on the altar in the Chapel of the Holy Souls, with Rosso Antico on the floor below.

11. Grand Antique des Pyrénées

There are a dozen different varieties of French marble in the Cathedral, mostly in shades of red or green. But certainly the most striking, and perhaps the most attractive, consists of almost equal proportions of sharply contrasting jet black and snow white. Grand Antique des Pyrénées is consequently known as Bianco-e-Nero (white and black) and was used by the Romans, the Byzantines and then, in more recent times, by the French.

Grand Antique marble column outside the Vaughan Chantry in the Cathedral

The marble can be seen on entering the Cathedral, forming the pedestal for the statue of St Peter which was made in Rome in 1901-2. On the floor nearby is another black and white marble. But this one, Grand Antique de Belgique, from Namur, is essentially black (indicating the presence of carbon), the white consisting only of veining. At the other end of the Cathedral, framed panels of French Grand Antique can be found on the walls of the Lady Chapel apse and it also appears on two of the nave piers at gallery level, but it can best be seen in the two black and white columns outside the Vaughan Chantry in the north transept, installed in 1907.

The marble quarry lies close to the village of Aubert, Ariège, in the French Midi-Pyrénées. Here the Route St Jacques (the medieval pilgrim road to Santiago de Compostela) runs beside the river Lez and it is on the track beside this river, about three miles south-west of St Girons, that the quarry is found. The remains now consist of roofless buildings made of blocks of the marble, rusting machinery for cutting and lifting the blocks and a mournful, motionless, silent lake, surrounded by trees and carpeted with water weed – the quarry itself, now flooded. Known in dialect as the Trau de Debremberi and in French as the Trou de l'Oubli (the chasm of oblivion in English), it is to be approached with caution.

The marble extends into the nearby river bed and can be seen on the path which runs alongside the river to the next village of Moulis, about a mile away. Besides its official title, the marble was locally nicknamed Grand Deuil (deep mourning) when it was predominantly black, and Petit Deuil when predominantly white. It was formed about 100 million years ago in the Lower Cretaceous period when the original black, carbonaceous, fossil limestone was fragmented by earth movements and then combined with pure white calcite to produce the unique juxtaposition of black and white that can be seen today.

The quarry village of Aubert.

Known to the Romans as Marmor Celticum, discoveries near the quarry include a Latin inscription, artefacts and coins, including a gold Valentinian of the later 4th century, indicating that the marble was being exploited by the Romans by that time.

The sign at the quarry.

This is confirmed by recycled examples in the Basilica of St Peter, St Mary Major, Santa Cecilia in Trastevere and elsewhere in Rome. The marble can also be found in the 6th century Basilica of Sant'Apollinare in Classe in Ravenna and in Emperor Justinian's great Byzantine church of Santa Sophia in Istanbul, being described by Justinian's court poet when the church reopened in 563 as 'the product of the Celtic crags, a wealth of crystals, like milk poured here and there on a flesh of glittering black' To get there from Aubert it must have travelled 2,000 miles.

For hundreds of years after Roman exploitation the quarry lay abandoned and all knowledge of its locality was forgotten. The only examples available were those which had been quarried centuries before. Thus the six columns at the main entrance of St Mark's, Venice (with others inside) may well have been looted from Constantinople by the 4th Crusaders in 1204. French writers on marbles described the quarry as lost both in 1720 (Daviller) and in 1808 (Brard). It was rediscovered in 1844 and vigorously worked from 1876, when the use of marble for decoration on a grand scale had been made fashionable by the opening of the Opéra Garnier in Paris the previous year. It finally closed in 1948.

There are many examples of this attractive marble to be seen in France – three columns in the Roman baths at the Cluny Museum in Paris, around Napoleon's tomb in the Dome Church at Les Invalides, decorating the Opéra Garnier and as pedestals in the Salon de Diane at the Palace of Versailles. Like most marbles it has also been used locally – for the altar in Moulis church, for panelling a shop in St Girons, for columns at Tarbes Cathedral and for shelves and a table in the main post office at Toulouse.

Britain also had impressive examples. It was used at Windsor Castle for the sarcophagus of the Prince Consort together with wall panels and the altar in the Albert Chapel (installed in 1870). In London it was used in Salisbury House and the Holborn restaurant and for six imposing columns and piers in the entrance hall of the Metropole Hotel – completed in 1885 at the bottom of Northumberland Avenue, but now a government building with security gates which partially obscure the columns. Sadly, of these locations the Metropole building is now inaccessible, Salisbury House and the Holborn restaurant no longer exist and the Albert Chapel requires an entrance fee. So that just leaves Westminster Cathedral.

Twisted columns of Grand Antique support the baldacchino at Les Invalides in Paris.

12. Campan

The Campan quarry, now abandoned, at Espiadet in the French Pyrenees.

Campan marble is a multi-coloured, variegated limestone first discovered by the Romans and used extensively in France during the Renaissance and in more recent times. It has been widely used in the Cathedral.

After their occupation of Transalpine Gaul, the Romans used Campan marble or Cipollino Mandalato, as it was also called, from the 1st century BC to the Byzantine period, and exported it to Rome and elsewhere (including Britain) particularly in and after the Severan period (193-238 AD). Since then it has continued to be employed in churches and elsewhere throughout the Pyrenees and, from the time of Louis XIV, has been widely used in royal and aristocratic buildings such as the Palaces of Versailles and Fontainebleau, the Louvre and the new (1875) Paris Opera House. Quarrying has continued until relatively recently and Campan marble was one of the main marbles used to decorate Westminster Cathedral.

A block of Campan Rouge at the quarry.

Campan marble is a fossil-rich limestone formed in the Devonian period about 350 million years ago in the Hautes-Pyrénées region of south-west France. The main quarry is at Espiadet which lies beside the road near the village of Payolle in the Campan river valley - some 20 miles south-east of Lourdes. The quarry contains marbles of many colours ranging from white to grey, pink, deep red and green, often all contained in the same block. As a result Campan marbles are referred to by their colour and appearance. Many have been listed over the years, those generally accepted being Campan Vert (the most common), Campan Rose et Vert (or Rosé Vert), Campan Rouge, Campan Rubané (ribboned), Campan Mélangé (mixed) and Campan Isabelle.

After the Roman and Byzantine periods it was not until the 17th century and under Louis XIV in particular that coloured marble from France came back into favour, not least to save on the cost of imported Italian marble. Several ancient French marble quarries were reopened, including the Campan quarry at Espiadet and all were reserved for the King. Louis XIV liked both the red and green varieties of Campan and is recorded as ordering 81 cubic feet of Campan Vert as early as 1669 for tables, fireplaces and foyers in many of the royal palaces. He also built up large stocks of Campan marble in the royal warehouses and it was these that his successors Louis XV and Louis XVI subsequently employed for projects such as the decoration of the floor at the Chateau de Fontainebleau and for the Queen's staircase at Versailles. Cardinal Richelieu also had a table made of the marble.

The quarry at Espiadet is relatively easy to work, being located on the side of a mountain close to a road, but transport overland to the junction of the Neste and Garonne rivers at Montrejeau was laborious and costly. To avoid this Louis XIV's Minister, Louvois, had the marble blocks hauled by oxen up over the Béyréde mountains. From there the marble blocks could slide down the other side to the Neste river – a more direct route which saved 90% of the cost of land transport. Both here and elsewhere the cost of transport was all-important. Thus a cubic foot of Campan Vert marble in 1765 was worth just 13 livres (£1.40) at the quarry but by the time it had travelled over the mountains, down the river to Bordeaux, then by sea to Le Havre and finally up the Seine to the Paris warehouses it would be worth 45 livres – a three- to four-fold increase.

Two varieties of Campan marble above the Baptistry screen in the Cathedral.

In Westminster Cathedral Campan marbles were first used by the firm of J Whitehead & Sons to decorate the Chapel of St Gregory and St Augustine in 1902. Here, projecting either side of the altarpiece and on the wall opposite adjoining the Baptistry, are great panels of Campan Rouge, Campan Vert and Campan Mélangé (red and green), while above the gates (on both sides) panels of Campan Rouge enclose diamonds of Campan Rose et Vert. Campan Mélangé also appears in the inner crypt above Cardinal Manning's tomb, while Campan Vert can be seen on the baldacchino and elsewhere in the sanctuary, in the nave aisles, passages and transepts and in seven of the twelve chapels. It was last used from 1956-64 to decorate the aisle piers (those bearing the First, Third, Fifth, Tenth, Twelfth and Fourteenth Stations of the Cross). Elsewhere in London, columns of Campan Vert can be found in the foyer of the Hotel Russell (built 1900) in Bloomsbury's Russell Square.

13. Connemara Green

The green marble of Connemara is an ophicalcite, extremely varied both in colour and pattern. It is known as Connemara Green or Irish Green. It is also very old. It comes from quarries in the neighbourhood of Clifden, the capital of Connemara, and its history is interwoven with the history and development of that town.

A block of marble at Streamstown quarry.

Connemara Green marble was originally a lime mud formed in shallow seas in the Pre-Cambrian period, some 600 million years ago or more. About 100 million years later it was metamorphosed, recrystallized under immense heat and pressure, and new minerals such as serpentine, chlorite and mica developed. It is these minerals that give the marble its characteristic and attractive variety of patterns and colours - a unique combination of bands, veins and patches of green, yellow, brown, white and grey.

Marble from Streamstown quarry on the front of the altar in St Patrick's Chapel.

In 1804, John D'Arcy, aged only 19, inherited large estates in Connemara, then largely cut off from the outside world. He described his tenants as 'a rare breed of people, wild like the mountains they inhabit'. By 1812 he had resolved to establish a town and seaport there, with roads linking it to Galway and Westport. From his new home in Clifden Castle, west of Clifden, he badgered the government in Dublin Castle for money to relieve local poverty and unemployment by building piers and roads, while offering permanent leases of land to those prepared to settle in the area. By 1826 a prosperous modern town had been created at Clifden, trading directly with Liverpool and elsewhere.

Meanwhile, two miles north of Clifden, close to the turn-off for the Sky Road and Streamstown Bay, John D'Arcy was developing a small quarry of banded dark and light green marble. From Streamstown the marble blocks were carted by a new road to Clifden for shipment from the newly-built pier. On his death in 1839, John's son, Hyacinth, continued to work the quarry, but the Great Famine of 1845-9 ruined the family and resulted in the sale of their estates, including the quarry, to Thomas Eyre of Bath. Hyacinth D'Arcy joined the Church of Ireland and became Rector of Clifden, building a new church there in 1853.

By this time Connemara marble was becoming well known. In the early 1840's two English travellers, the Halls, wrote glowingly of it and purchased a slab measuring 3ft x 2ft for £3/10s. A book by Sir Robert Kane in 1844 referred to marble from the D'Arcy quarries at Streamstown being exported in considerable quantities. A few years later, in 1850, panels of Connemara were displayed in Dublin's Museum of Economic Geology, with columns in the Museum of Trinity College nearby, while in England columns of the marble were used for Oxford's University Museum of Natural History.

Barnanoraun quarry in the rain.

Clifden pier was used extensively until 1895, when a railway linked the town with Galway. In the same year Streamstown quarry was acquired by Robert Fisher of New York and large amounts of marble exported for American churches and public buildings. It was also much used in England - perhaps most extravagantly in the new General Post Office at King Edward's Buildings in the City of London, opened in 1910. More recently, in 1981, Pope John Paul II was presented with an 18in Celtic cross and candlesticks of Streamstown marble on behalf of the youth of Ireland. The light green, dark green and sepia varieties of Streamstown marble continue to be marketed by Connemara Marble Industries from its factory and showroom at Moycullen, near Galway City.

In the Cathedral, slabs of this green marble, with its attractive figuring, can be seen on the east wall, altar and floor of St Patrick's Chapel, and also on the floor of St Andrew's and the Baptistry. Celtic designs on the floor of St Patrick's, and leaves and wreaths on that in the Lady Chapel, show dark Streamstown alternating and contrasting with a yellower marble which may be from Barnanoraun quarry. This lies in the Owenglin valley, six miles east of Clifden, and the marble there has wilder and more tangled patterns than that of Streamstown. The yellowish-green panels on the floor of the Vaughan Chantry may also be from Barnanoraun.

Barnanoraun quarry formed part of the estate of the Martins of Ballynahinch Castle and the marble, also called Ballynahinch marble, was carted the five miles over a steep ridge down to Ballynahinch and Cloonisle pier for shipment. The quarry has been in operation from at least the early nineteenth century, its marble being described by Sir C L Giesecke to the Royal Dublin Society in 1826. It also appears in the museum buildings of Trinity College and Oxford University. Today Joyce's Marble Quarries markets blocks, gallets, slabs and tiles of Barnanoraun marble from a factory at Recess, twelve miles down the road from Clifden, and a nearby craft shop sells carved marble articles to visitors.

Probably the most beautiful example of Connemara marble in the Cathedral appears in the centre of the altar frontal in St Joseph's Chapel. This translucent, clouded green panel is almost identical to sample 88 in the Sedgwick Museum of Geology in Cambridge which comes from Lissoughter quarry on the south-west slope of Lissoughter Hill, just above Recess. Other examples in the Cathedral are the light green diamonds high on the walls of the Lady Chapel. Elsewhere in London, Lissoughter green decorated the old hotel and booking office of St Pancras Station. Originally worked to a small extent by the Martins of Ballynahinch, in 1870 the Dublin firm of Sibthorpe took over and began extensive production. The quarry is currently owned by J C Walsh. But despite the beauty of the marble, it is troublesome to work and the quarry is now used only occasionally to produce random blocks for tiles and giftware.

A panel of Irish Green from Lissoughter quarry, surrounded by Yellow Siena, decorates the altar in St Joseph's Chapel.

14. Cork Red

There are at least four Irish marbles in Westminster Cathedral. Of these by far the most prominent is the mottled red marble which can be seen on the back wall above the wooden cabinets, behind the Information Desk, on the inner face of the nave piers and in many of the chapels – notably St Patrick's. Although the Cathedral was far from the first to use it, it was almost certainly the last.

Cork Red comes from County Cork in Ireland. It is an unusual and attractive limestone made up of pebbles, some grey but most stained varying shades of red by iron oxide, set in a deeper red matrix. A range of fossils can be seen, mainly crinoids (sea-lilies), but also other marine creatures such as molluscs. It was formed in the Lower Carboniferous period (about 300 million years ago) when a grey limestone reef beneath the warm, shallow sea then covering the region was buried beneath red sediment, carried by currents or perhaps resulting from a tilting of the sea floor.

Victoria Red on the altar in St Patrick's Chapel with crinoid fossils much in evidence.

Cork Red marble was quarried near Fermoy and Buttevant, at Midleton and nearby Baneshane, and at Boreenmanagh, Churchtown and Little Island close to Cork City. The marble was known by 1850, when examples (still on show) were displayed in the foyer of the Museum of Economic Geology in Dublin. From then on it was used to decorate many important buildings such as the Museum of Trinity College in Dublin, the Oxford University Natural History Museum, the Liverpool and Manchester Exchanges, St Finbarre's Cathedral in Cork, and St Colman's in Cobh, both of which possess great columns of the marble. But World War I and the Troubles disrupted both building and trade and the Cork Red quarries, by then largely exhausted, fell into disuse.

Westminster Cathedral has the marble in the nave and the inner crypt and also on the floor of the sanctuary, the Lady Chapel (either side of the altar) and near the niches outside the Blessed Sacrament Chapel. The altar table in the Sacred Heart Shrine is also of Cork Red while in St Patrick's Chapel it can be seen in the altar frontal (a particularly attractive deep red variety called Victoria Red after Queen Victoria), the floor and the little columns lining the wall below the windows. All the marble appears to be from the same source. Geological Survey of Ireland records show that Cork Red from Baneshane Quarry was used in the Cathedral about 1910. Farmer & Brindley, of Westminster Bridge Road, were responsible for the marblework in the Cathedral at that time and are likely to have used only one quarry for the Cork Red they needed. They returned in the 1920s to lay the floor and erect the columns in St Patrick's Chapel, probably using pre-war stock.

Baneshane quarry, 180ft long, 40ft wide and 15ft deep, lies in the County Cork countryside, twelve miles to the east of Cork City and one mile west of the market town of Midleton. Open by 1850, in 1914 it seems to have been abandoned and allowed to fill with water which was used to irrigate local fields. But in early 1956, after much discussion in the Cathedral Art Committee, it was resolved that the nave of the Cathedral should be clad with marble in line with the original designs. By now Farmer & Brindley were no more and the marble merchants chosen, J Whitehead & Sons of Kennington Oval, recommended a salmon-pink Portuguese marble for the red needed.

It was Aelred Bartlett, artist and brother of Francis, the future Administrator of the Cathedral, who rejected this proposal and who approached the Irish Embassy in London to see if Cork Red marble was still obtainable. With the help of the Geological Survey of Ireland, Aelred travelled to Baneshane quarry on 12 April 1956. The quarry was inspected, drained and reopened and, from 1956-64, the Cathedral nave and narthex received its marble cladding, including the Cork Red last put in place 30 years before – the red of Baneshane. Since then, despite the potential for further development, the quarry has again been abandoned, overgrown with briars, gorse and maturing trees. Now forgotten by almost all, at least it will be remembered in Westminster Cathedral.

Cork Red inlaid with a Celtic design on the floor of St Patrick's Chapel.

15. Kilkenny Black

Kilkenny marble in St Patrick's Chapel.

We have already described two well known Irish marbles which we have in the Cathedral - Cork Red and Connemara Green. We now look at a third - Kilkenny Black - which can be found on the altar table, altarpiece and floor in St Patrick's Chapel.

Although listed when it was installed by the marble merchants Farmer & Brindley in 1910 (1928 in the case of the floor) simply as black Irish fossil marble, it is believed to come from what may well be Ireland's oldest marble quarry - the Black Quarry beside the River Nore near Archer's Grove, about half a mile south-east of the city of Kilkenny which is known as the Marble City. The marble is a limestone formed from the remains of a myriad of marine organisms which lived and died about 300 million years ago when warm, shallow seas covered much of Britain and Ireland. This accounts for the presence of a variety of marine fossils, characteristic of Kilkenny marble and clearly discernible on the altar in St Patrick's Chapel.

Dr Gerald Boate, writing in 1652, refers to the widespread use of the marble for house building and paving in Kilkenny and states that the nearby quarry 'belongeth to nobody in particular'. But in 1730 Alderman William Colles of Patrick Street took a perpetual lease on it having successfully invented machinery to cut, bore and polish marble by means of waterpower. In fact he was the first person to use water to bore and polish marble and the first to use it for sawing stone since the Romans. The marble blocks were carted from the Black Quarry over Kilkenny bridge and then three miles downstream to Maddockstown where Colles's watermill undertook the work of 42 men a day, cutting and polishing a wide variety of chimney-pieces, tables, punch-bowls etc which were displayed in on-site warehouses. Up to 100 tons of marble a year was also exported in rough blocks to Liverpool and Glasgow via the seaport at Waterford.

William Colles also invented machines for dressing flax and for weaving linen by dog-power, and a floating musical instrument activated by the movement of the river. Local gossip had it that he was a necromancer. His attempts to reduce transport costs by building a canal beside the river ended when government funds ran out but the marble works continued to be a commercial success. William Colles died in 1770 and was succeeded by a further four generations of the family who built a paper mill and grain mill further downstream and ran the marble works until 1920 when Richard Colles finally retired and sold out after 44 years in charge.

Colles's marble sawing mill beside the River Nore.

By then it had become the Irish Marble Company, Kilkenny and included other marble quarries elsewhere such as one of Connemara Green, another of Cork Red and Butler's Grove Quarry, ten miles due east of Kilkenny City. This still produces a pure black marble which was used for the Chapel of the Seven Dolours in Brompton Oratory and is very similar to that from the Black Quarry. But production at Butler's Grove is now only for road-building.

Unlike Butler's Grove, the Black Quarry now stands silent. The new owners continued production for some time after 1920 but the effects of the 1914-18 War, the Troubles and then Economic Depression disrupted commerce and trade patterns and the trend in demand was away from the use of decorative marble. Today the quarry is bisected by the busy R700 main road and modern housing estates encroach on all sides but the river. On the upper level, Gallows Hill, a service station occupies much of the quarry site. The lower, between the road and the River Nore, lies overgrown and abandoned with only the rusting buckets and boom of a crane and disintegrating oil drums as a reminder of its long history. Two miles downstream the old marble sawing mill stands in ruins amidst the trees beside the river, its machinery and water wheel long gone but the fragments of marble which surround it pointing to its past.

But of course both the Black Quarry and William Colles's watermill live on in the marble they produced. Many of the houses, walls and pavements of Kilkenny are made of it, as is the chancel pavement of the local Cathedral, St Canice. Columns of Kilkenny Black stand in Oxford University's Natural History Museum and in the museum at Dublin's Trinity College, while it can also be seen in the old Parliament Building on College Green. Appropriately enough it was used for the tomb of Daniel O'Connell, himself a friend of the Colles family, in Glasnevin Cemetery. In 1928, when the time came to restore Dublin's GPO building, gutted in the 1916 Easter Rising, the marbles chosen were Ireland's most famous - Cork Red, Connemara Green and Kilkenny Black - the same Irish marbles which we have in Westminster Cathedral.

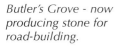

Butler's Grove - now producing stone for road-building.

16. Iona Green

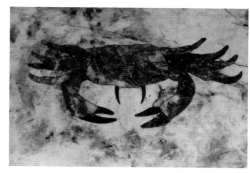

Iona Green marble inlaid with crab on the floor of St Andrew's Chapel in the Cathedral.

One of the most unusual of the Cathedral's marbles is Scottish, from a tiny quarry, long disused, on the island of Iona in the Hebrides. Iona Green marble can be seen on the floor of the Chapel of St Andrew, patron saint of Scotland. It is predominantly white, flecked with light and dark green, and is inlaid here with twenty-nine fish and other marine creatures. The marble was put in place in 1913-15 by the firm of Farmer & Brindley at the expense of the Fourth Marquess of Bute.

Geologically, Iona Green is a true marble in which the original limestone has been recrystallised (metamorphosed) under great heat and pressure. The quarry lies almost at the southernmost point of Iona, in a valley beside the sea just to the east of St Columba's Bay. Translucent green pebbles of the marble are thrown up by the sea in nearby bays and are known as 'mermaids tears', from the legend that a match between a mermaid and an Iona monk was prevented by King Neptune and the Abbot.

By the end of the 17th century writers were referring to a marble altar table in Iona Abbey, on the other side of the island. This was destroyed in the 18th century as a

The altar in Iona Abbey.

result of a local belief that possession of a fragment would protect against shipwrecks, fire and miscarriages, but today both the modern altar table and the font base are of Iona Green marble. In the late 18th century quarrying again took place, organised by the Duke of Argyll, and quantities of marble were sent to Leith and London before extraction and transport problems put an end to the venture. It seems probable that intermittent quarrying of Iona Green has occurred from at least medieval times.

The marble for St Andrew's Chapel was quarried by the Iona Marble Company, formed in 1906. This operated with up to twelve men until the 1914-18 War and the loss of the Belgian market put a stop to operations. The Secretary of the Company went off to fight and many of the quarrymen will have done the same. So there the quarry lies today, scattered blocks and fragments of marble, cutting machinery for slabs, and footings for the derricks which used to swing the marble onto Glasgow-bound vessels, all now frozen in time.

The quarry in Iona as it lies today, idle rusting machinery with scattered blocks and fragments of marble.

17. Derbyshire Fossil and Hopton Wood

Perhaps surprisingly, of all the marbles in Westminster Cathedral, only two come from England and Wales. These are Derbyshire Fossil and Hopton Wood, limestones originally laid down in shallow tropical seas in what today is the Peak District of Derbyshire.

Derbyshire fossil marble is used for the skirting at the entrance to St Andrew's Chapel.

The two marbles are composed of fragments of marine life such as shells, corals and animal debris, which gradually accumulated on the sea floor to a depth of thousands of feet. At that time, in the Carboniferous Period some 330 million years ago, Britain was 5°-10° south of the Equator, rather than 50° degrees north as today, and the region would have looked like a series of Pacific Ocean reefs surrounding a lagoon.

The most attractive example of Derbyshire Fossil marble in the Cathedral is the skirting between St Paul's and St Andrew's Chapels. Light grey in colour, it contains an abundance of fossilised sea creatures, notably crinoids. These sea-lilies consist of a flower-like structure supported by a jointed stem attached to the sea floor. A series of hard rings surround and protect the stem and these, sometimes called 'St Cuthbert's Beads' and used to make rosaries, can be seen clearly. When the marble is dark the white rings stand out, resembling the eye of a bird - hence 'Bird's-eye marble'. The lighter example here in the Cathedral appears to be from 'Once-a-week' quarry at Monyash, so named because the local hunt met there once a week. The quarry was in operation at least as early as the 16th century and its marble was used extensively for decorating Chatsworth House which owns the land where the quarry stands. It remains in production today.

A less likely source for the light grey fossil marble in the Cathedral is Dene quarry in Dene Hollow on the outskirts of Cromford (where Arkwright had his mill). But commercial production here really only started in 1942, after this marble is believed to have been installed in the Cathedral. By the 1960s production difficulties at Dene quarry and reduced demand for decorative fossil marble had resulted in a concentration on the mass production of crushed stone for road-building, which continues today.

The other examples of Derbyshire Fossil in the Cathedral are darker. A brown variety with less obvious fossils is used for the column bases and retaining walls either side of the sanctuary. Then some fifty years ago, from 1956-64, the nave piers and narthex received their marble cladding and, once again, dark Derbyshire Fossil was chosen for the skirting. This is an almost black variety which appears to come either from Steeplehouse (Smart's) quarry or from Coal Hills quarry, both near Wirksworth. Steeplehouse also produced Birds-eye marble and operated from the 1930s to the 1970s. Coal Hills, which was also a source of tarred macadam from the 1820s to the 1930s, is now owned by the National Stone Centre.

Dene quarry - now producing crushed stone for road-building.

Like Derbyshire Fossil, Hopton Wood marble is used extensively in the Cathedral. It ranges from a rich cream to a dark grey or fawn, depending on its position in the quarry and the number of fossils, largely crinoids. Of uniform texture it is a compact stone of great hardness which can be used internally and externally. It was first extracted at Hopton Wood in the mid-18th century and employed extensively for flooring and staircases in the rebuilding of Kedleston Hall near Derby in the 1760s and 1770s. To cope with increasing demand for what became a fashionable stone, quarries were opened at nearby Middleton, close to Wirksworth, where production was centred.

In the Cathedral, Hopton Wood marble is seen in the arches either side of the sanctuary and around the reliquaries and windows in the crypt. In St Paul's Chapel the two piscinas, put in place either side of the altar in 1914-15, are also of this marble, decorated with red and white inlay and given a high polish. In the aisles near the Cathedral entrance the holy water stoups, each surmounted by a carved shell and dating from 1918, demonstrate that Hopton Wood is virtually impervious to water. Here they have been given a light 'eggshell' polish. And, as if to demonstrate its versatility, the same marble, inlaid with red and green porphyry this time, was laid on the floor of St Joseph's Chapel in 1939.

But the best known Hopton Wood marble in the Cathedral is undoubtedly that used for the Stations of the Cross. Eric Gill used stone of various types for his sculptures, among them Bath, Beer and Portland. But Hopton Wood seems to have been his favourite. He is recorded as taking his apprentices up to Wirksworth to select blocks, and both at the start and at the end of his career he used Hopton Wood - for the Cathedral stations in 1914-18 and for the altarpiece in St George's Chapel in 1939-40. Appropriately enough, his memorial below the Fourteenth Station is also of Hopton Wood.

II. JESUS RECEIVES HIS CROSS

The Stations of the Cross in the Cathedral are of carved light Hopton Wood.

So why were British marbles not used more extensively in the Cathedral? Why do we not have the green of Anglesey, the red and white of Plymouth and Totnes, the swirling red-black and green of Cornish Lizard serpentine? Firstly, because the Cathedral is in the Byzantine style and many of the marbles here are those used in Byzantine churches. Secondly, the main marble decorator for the Cathedral, William Brindley, had personally located and reopened ancient quarries in Greece and elsewhere and wanted to exploit them. And finally, because of differing production and transport costs, it was quite simply cheaper to import Continental marble by sea than to raise and convey marble from British quarries by train.

18. Gerontius and Princess Blue

In 2003 two inlaid marble panels were installed at the entrance to the Holy Souls Chapel. They commemorate the first London performance in 1903 of 'The Dream of Gerontius', written by Cardinal Newman and set to music by Edward Elgar. The nine marbles used increased the total number employed in the Cathedral from 124 to 126 (with three more unidentified) and, with the addition of Morocco, raised the number of countries from which they came from 24 to 25.

The Gerontius panel at the entrance to the Holy Souls Chapel.

The panels were designed by Tom Phillips and made by Taylor Pearce of London using marbles supplied by McMarmilloyd of Great Bedwyn in Wiltshire. Starting with the left-hand panel and working inwards from the original veined white Carrara marble frame, there is Princess Blue from Ontario, Canada (dark blue); Lido from Tiflet, near Rabat in Morocco (grey brown); Rosso Levanto from Liguria in Italy (veined dark red); Crema Valencia from Valencia in Spain (pink flushed cream); Verde di Mare from near Genoa in Italy (veined dark green); and finally pure white Carrara from Tuscany.

The marbles used for the right-hand panel are largely the same except that the light green is Swedish Green from Norrkoping, the yellow is Siena from Tuscany and the red-brown is Brèche de Kleber from Oran Province in Algeria. The fact that the panels employ only two new marbles is intentional. All except Moroccan Lido and Crema Valencia were previously used to decorate the walls and floor of the Holy Souls Chapel (Carrara, Princess Blue, Rosso Levanto and Verde di Mare) or nearby St George's Chapel (Swedish Green). Crema Valencia is closely related to the

Spanish Pink (Rosa Valencia) marble there, and they come from the same quarries near Barxeta in Valencia. Yellow Siena marble decorates the altar frontal in St Joseph's Chapel.

The most interesting of the marbles used is Princess Blue, also known as 'Canadian Blue' (as in the Holy Souls' Chapel) and 'Alomite' after Charles Allom of White, Allom and Co who first introduced it into Britain. In the Cathedral it can be seen in the coat of arms of the Walmsley family (who paid for the chapel decoration) on the floor of the Holy Souls Chapel. A brilliant blue sodalite, interspersed with thin red veins and patches, the marble beds in the quarries at Bancroft, Ontario, lie together with spurs and pockets of granite and mica, making it both difficult and expensive to extract.

When the future King George V and Queen Mary visited Canada at the beginning of the 20th century, Princess Mary was much struck by the beauty of the blue marble shown to her. It was named 'Princess Blue', and the quarries from which it came were named 'Princess Quarries', in her honour. As a result of her interest the marble, the first from the colonies, was exported to this country in 1905. Indeed the Cathedral must have been among the first to use it since the marble floor in the Holy Souls Chapel was laid shortly afterwards, in the Spring of 1906, by J Whitehead & Sons of Kennington Oval.

Princess Blue in the Walmsley coat of arms on the floor of the Holy Souls Chapel.

EXPLORING THE QUARRIES A PERSONAL ODYSSEY

Statuary marble quarry in the mist, Monte Altissimo, Tuscany.

Exploring the Quarries - A Personal Odyssey

I first became interested in the Westminster Cathedral marbles on joining the Cathedral as a volunteer and guide in 1992. But I soon came to realize that, despite some work which Francis Bartlett had done when Sub-Administrator in the 1950s, the only systematic description of the marbles dated from 1919. Since then the number had more than doubled and many of the new varieties had gone

The signpost for the quarries (complete with 16 bullet holes), Profitis Ilias, the Mani.

unrecorded. Clearly the first task was to produce a comprehensive list of what we had and where they came from. The first draft of this was completed in 1995 and I was then able to start to research the history of our marbles and explore the quarries from which they had come, a task facilitated by a career in research and analysis and army training in the use of map and compass.

The first trip was in 1997 and was relatively straightforward, though the journey took twelve hours – by train from London to Glasgow and on to Oban, then by ferry across to Mull, bus across the island and finally another ferry to Iona. Nevertheless there was still quite a sense of achievement the next day, after walking across the island to St Columba's Bay and scrambling down a nearby valley to the sea, to be standing surrounded by marble blocks and abandoned quarry machinery last used by the men of the Iona Marble Company in 1914.

The next project was more difficult. It involved a good deal of research and also introduced me to the dangers of dehydration. The trip, in the year 2000, was to the ancient Rosso Antico quarries in the largely deserted area of Greece known as the Mani. The first sight of this red marble, after a long walk over the hills, was of a strange pink glow against the dark blue of the sea at a cove called Paganea, so I took a chance and headed straight for it. The only problem was that, after spending too long exploring the workings, I then had to climb back up through the hills weighed down with marble samples and with very little water left. It was extremely hot, the few inhabitants must have been asleep so no chance of a lift, and I had to catch the one and only school bus in the next village. When I got there I drained two litres of water in one vast swallow.

Carrying enough water is a constant problem as walking distances can be long, the Mediterranean sun extremely hot and you normally want to bring back a few hand samples of marble from the quarries. But in Connemara in Ireland in 2002 the problem was too much, rather than not enough, water. It rained solidly the whole day with a steady determination to really soak you through to the skin. A 'soft day' as it is known. Actually it is ideal for looking at, and photographing, marble as all the colours stand out just as if the rock had been polished, so the swirling green

Espiadet quarry and the Campan Valley, Hautes-Pyrénées, France.

and yellow Connemara Green marble at Barnanoraun quarry looked really spectacular. Another spectacular but very wet place was Monte Altissimo in Tuscany, Italy, where Michelangelo found much of his marble. The mist was eddying and swirling all around me frustrating any attempt to find a landmark. It was only when it finally cleared that I was able to see where I was.

A different type of hazard awaited at the Cork Red marble quarry in Ireland. I knew exactly where the Cathedral marble had come from as a result of a Geological Survey of Ireland map. Against Baneshane quarry someone had written in longhand 'Inspected and sampled with Mr Bartlett, 12 April 1956'. Aelred Bartlett was from the Cathedral. It was only after my own visit to the quarry that I realized that I had been there on the same day almost fifty years later – 12 April 2002. Since being worked in 1956, the quarry has become heavily overgrown with trees and brambles and has a deep, concrete sided, trench at the bottom covered with rusting sheets of corrugated iron. Despite a real sense of foreboding I went back the next day and on the way was bitten on the ankle by a gypsy dog. So I abandoned the quarry and retraced my steps, this time equipped with a stick. The dog was now chained up and clearly thinking beautiful thoughts. But I looked back and it was gazing after me and grinning.

Two years later I met a much more friendly dog at the Verde Antico quarries on Mount Ossa near Larissa in Central Greece. I had climbed up to the quarrymen's church when I heard a bark behind me. Remembering the Baneshane incident I immediately resigned myself to being bitten again. But instead this dog, clearly the guardian of the quarries and the church, accompanied me all around the site, barking occasionally to point out something interesting. It gazed after me so mournfully when I finally had to leave. The problem there was not dogs but flies –

millions of them attracted by hundreds of tons of apricots which had been dumped just below the quarries (presumably grown just for the EEC subsidies). Clearly bored with apricots by this time they were on the lookout for a change of diet – me. They completely enveloped me - inside my anorak, all over my camera and even into my mouth, nose and ears. Only gradually did they realize that apricots were easier eating. Other animals encountered around quarries included a friendly tortoise at Paganea in Greece and a very large brown snake which I was only three inches from treading on while climbing Mount Ochi on Evia. I am not sure which of us was the more shocked but subsequent research in my 'Boys Book of Reptiles' suggested it was only a harmless Whip Snake. Another confrontation with a snake which caused a few anxious moments was at a separation trench in Cave di Cusa quarries in Sicily.

The guardian of the quarries, Mount Ossa, Thessaly.

Quarries can be strange and dangerous places and it is unwise to take chances. The Romans used convicts at many of them and deaths would not have been unusual. In researching Grand Antique des Pyrénées marble I read that the old Roman quarry in France had flooded and became a lake, had sheer sides and was known locally as 'Le Trou de l'Oubli' (the chasm of oblivion). I could not get that name out of my head and once there resolutely resisted the temptation to scramble round the steep wooded bank for a better view. I also remember spending several hours in the Roman quarry at Kylindroi on the Greek island of Evia, where ancient Cipollino columns still lie abandoned. Without warning a very high wind blew up the valley from the sea below. On one side of the quarry there is a steep face and on the other a sheer drop while the ground is covered with ancient marble chippings. Suddenly my Millennium cap (bought in Castelgandolfo) was torn off and carried straight up into the sky. I never saw it again. Then the marble chips under my feet began to move in the wind and I had the distinct feeling that this was not a good place to be. So I went down and as I did so the wind dropped. I had outstayed my welcome.

Falls of course are an occupational hazard and usually result in nothing more than a few bruises and scratches from brambles. For more than a century wire has been used by quarrymen with sand and water to cut the marble and is often found lying around in quarries to trip the unwary. The only serious fall I had resulted from tiredness and loss of concentration on Mount Pentelicon, about 12 miles from Athens. After several frustrating and exhausting hours looking for Spelia quarry which Pericles used to build the Parthenon, the mound of white Pentelic marble rubble I was climbing (one of many resulting from illegal quarrying over the last century which now cover the ancient workings) gave way under me. When I came to some time later I was lying very peacefully under some pine trees but completely unable to breathe. At first I thought I had broken my ribs but then, very slowly, my breath returned and I realized I had fallen about 30 feet, striking the ground first with my staff, then with my left leg (which took three months to recover) and only then with my chest. I was, in fact, extremely fortunate and by rights, as my doctor later forcefully pointed out, I should have been in a Greek hospital.

Another place for Greek temples and ancient quarries is Sicily, also renowned for its breathtaking mosaics. I had been warned about pickpockets and had an experience of this on the bus from Palermo to Monreale. When it finally arrived I was immediately sandwiched in by a group of men. After a few minutes I felt a faint movement at waist level and forcing a hand downwards encountered another hand, a child's hand, in my pocket. Abruptly it pulled away and the whole group got out at the next stop. In amongst them a child must have been concealed but I never saw it. I had been saved by the pockets of my walking trousers, nine of them with zips (all now open) - a pickpocket's nightmare - and the fact that the little money I was carrying happened to be in the last pocket to be rifled. A surreal experience and more than compensated for a few days later when, running low on water while walking through the Sicilian countryside, I stopped at an isolated house and asked if they could help. In response three generations of the family brought out not only water but also Coca Cola, beer, wine and something in a flask which nearly blew my head off. They were a lovely family and refused any payment point blank.

One of the most memorable experiences must be Mons Porphyrites, the Mountain of Smoke, in the Egyptian Eastern Desert - where the Romans quarried Purple Porphyry. We travelled there in 2006 in two 4-wheel-drive Land Cruisers after spending the morning in another Roman quarry, Mons Claudianus. So the sun was low in the sky as we finally left the sand dunes and drove squishing through the gravel up a ravine enclosed by mountains towards the quarries. By the time we arrived at the Roman settlement it was almost dusk and after a brief exploration we had just started back when one of the vehicles got trapped in the rocks. It was completely dark by the time it had been jacked out and I was secretly hoping we would have to spend the night there. But instead the Bedouin guides drove the vehicles at breakneck speed through the wadis and ravines and finally out into the desert. Twice in that journey of several hours as we bucketed along I said to myself

"You must always remember this". Finally emerging from an unmarked track onto the coastal road near Hurghada, all the mobile phones burst into life as the authorities tried to find out where on earth we were. It is illegal for foreigners to be in the desert after sunset without a special permit.

Other memories are of the young Greek taxi driver who drove me to Mount Ossa identifying in turn the great snow capped mountains beyond; another on Evia who drove straight up a track on Mount Ochi until we could go no further and the wheels spun in the gravel, and of the old couple who, when I came down from that mountain so tired I was swaying, took both my arms and led me down the road to Karystos. I remember a lady with a huge shopping basket talking to me on the bus to Saint Girons in the French Pyrenees; another tiny lady in Ireland with a face as lined as a walnut who told me about the lorries she had seen leaving Baneshane quarry in the 1950s (carrying the Cork Red marble for the Cathedral); a ruined 18th century marble cutting mill standing beside the fast flowing River Nore near Kilkenny; picking up a fresh orange that had fallen from an orange grove in front of me in Laconia and eating it beside the sea. I remember the breathtaking view over the plain to the coast and beyond from the Green Porphyry quarry on the Hill of Psephi, and so many other views from so many other marble quarries; and I remember my solitary companion, the guardian of the Verde Antico quarries in Thessaly, Greece.

Mons Claudianus quarry, Egyptian Eastern Desert.

These are just a few of the things which have occurred while exploring ancient marble quarries and for me they are good enough reasons for doing so. But the main reason may lie further back. When I was a small boy, growing up in a large Catholic family on the outskirts of Folkestone, we had a garden with a wall. Beyond the wall was a valley occupied by cows with a bog and a stream at the bottom winding its way from the North Downs down to the sea at Sandgate. On the other side of the valley stood Shorncliffe Camp, occupied by the army since Napoleonic times. Every day, unless school rudely intervened, we were through the parlour window (doors were for grown-ups and anyway the back door was permanently jammed), down the garden, over the wall and into the valley. From there we could turn left down the hill to Heritage Farm, Star and Garter Wood and the sea, or turn right past the gorse for 'Muddy Path', Cheriton and the Downs. We called it 'going over the wall', 'going adventuring' or simply 'exploring'. I always loved it. I think I always will.

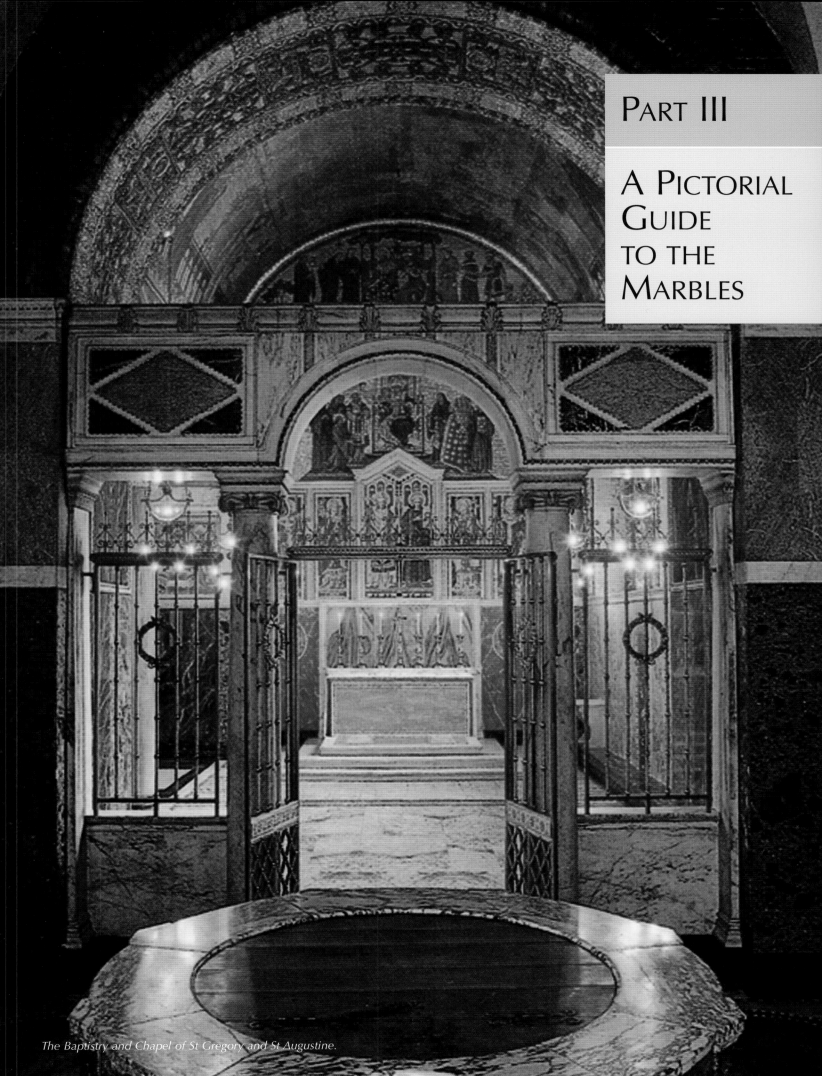

The Baptistry and Chapel of St Gregory and St Augustine.

1. THE NAVE

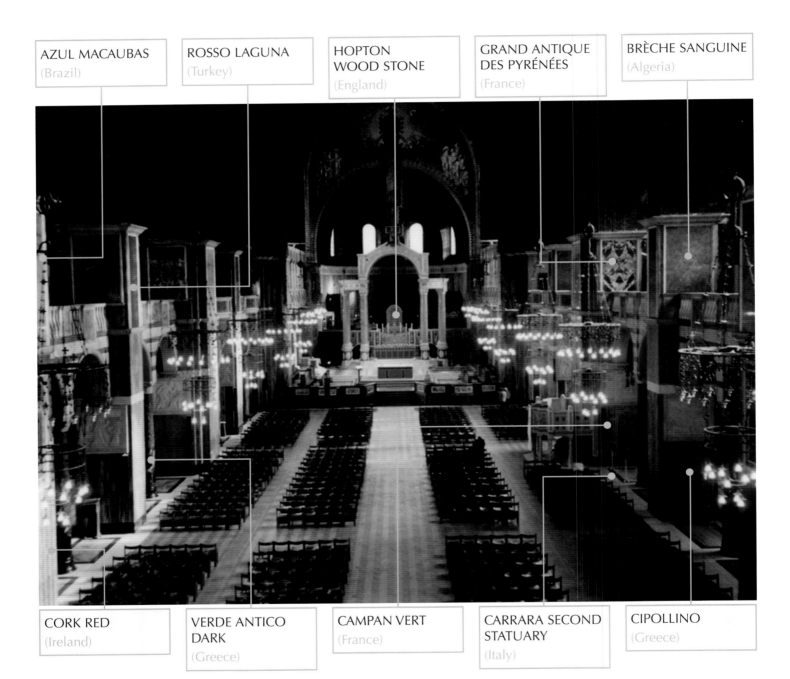

AZUL MACAUBAS
(Brazil)

ROSSO LAGUNA
(Turkey)

HOPTON
WOOD STONE
(England)

GRAND ANTIQUE
DES PYRÉNÉES
(France)

BRÈCHE SANGUINE
(Algeria)

CORK RED
(Ireland)

VERDE ANTICO
DARK
(Greece)

CAMPAN VERT
(France)

CARRARA SECOND
STATUARY
(Italy)

CIPOLLINO
(Greece)

2. THE SANCTUARY

RED VERONA
(ITALY)

PAVONAZZO
(ITALY)

ROUGE JASPÉ
(FRANCE)

CARRARA
STATUARY
(ITALY)

YELLOW VERONA
(ITALY)

BRÈCHE
ORIENTALE
(FRANCE)

NORWEGIAN PINK
(NORWAY)

BRECCIA
VIOLETTA
(ITALY)

ROSSO
ANTICO
(GREECE)

SIENA
BRECCIA
(ITALY)

3. THE BAPTISTRY AND CHAPEL OF ST GREGORY AND ST AUGUSTINE

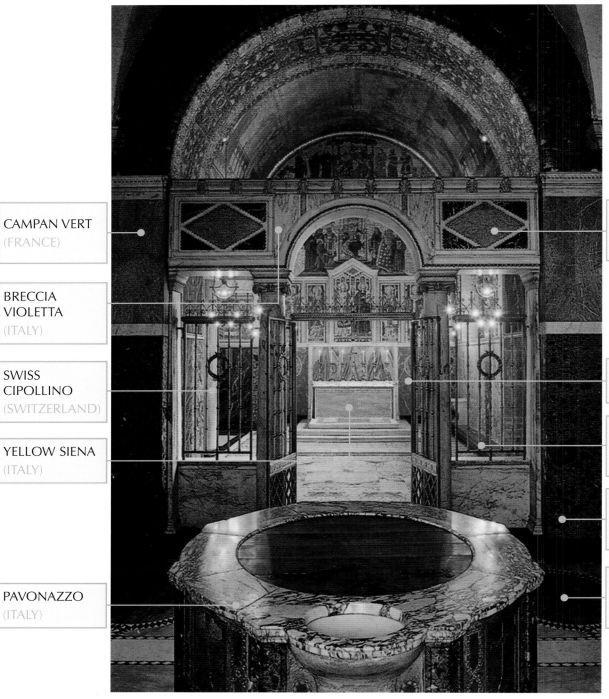

CAMPAN VERT
(FRANCE)

BRECCIA
VIOLETTA
(ITALY)

SWISS
CIPOLLINO
(SWITZERLAND)

YELLOW SIENA
(ITALY)

PAVONAZZO
(ITALY)

CAMPAN ROSE
ET VERT
(FRANCE)

ROUGE JASPÉ
(FRANCE)

ROSSO
LEVANTO
(ITALY)

VERDE ANTICO
PALE
(GREECE)

CONNEMARA
GREEN
(IRELAND)

4. THE CHAPEL OF ST PATRICK AND THE SAINTS OF IRELAND

YELLOW
VERONA
(ITALY)

VERDE ALPI
(ITALY)

ITALIAN
CIPOLLINO
(ITALY)

VICTORIA
RED
(IRELAND)

LAPIS LAZULI
(CHILE)

SKYROS
BRECCIA
(GREECE)

EMPEROR'S
RED
(PORTUGAL)

GREEN
SMARAGDITE
(CORSICA)

CONNEMARA
GREEN
(IRELAND)

GREEN VERDITE
(S. AFRICA)

5. THE CHAPEL OF ST ANDREW AND THE SAINTS OF SCOTLAND

PURPLE
PORPHYRY
(EGYPT)

ALLOA
GRANITE
(SCOTLAND)

PETERHEAD
GRANITE
(SCOTLAND)

ABERDEEN
GRANITE
(SCOTLAND)

IONA GREEN
(SCOTLAND)

GIALLO
ANTICO
(TUNISIA)

OLD
CIPOLLINO
(GREECE)

BLUE
HYMETTIAN
(GREECE)

WHITE
PENTELIC
(GREECE)

FANTASTICO
VIOLA
(ITALY)

6. THE CHAPEL OF ST PAUL

GREY
HYMETTIAN
(GREECE)

GREEN TINOS
(GREECE)

CIPOLLINO
(GREECE)

CAMPAN VERT
(FRANCE)

WHITE
PENTELIC
(GREECE)

PROCONNESIAN
(TURKEY)

ITALIAN
CIPOLLINO
(ITALY)

HOPTON
WOOD STONE
(ENGLAND)

PURPLE
PORPHYRY
(EGYPT)

PAVONAZZO
(ITALY)

7. THE LADY CHAPEL

CAMPAN VERT
(FRANCE)

PINK PAVONAZZO
(ITALY)

PURPLE VEINED
SIENA
(ITALY)

GRAND ANTIQUE
DES PYRÉNÉES
(FRANCE)

PURPLE BRECCIA
(ITALY)

VERDE ANTICO
PALE
(GREECE)

BRÈCHE
UNIVERSELLE
(EGYPT)

ROSSO ANTICO
(GREECE)

GIALLO ANTICO
(ALGERIA)

CIPOLLINO
(GREECE)

8. THE CHAPEL OF THE HOLY SOULS

PAVONAZZO
(ITALY)

DARK DOVE
(ITALY)

ROSSO LEVANTO
(ITALY)

VERT DES ALPES
(FRANCE)

BRÈCHE VERTE
(ITALY)

GREEN GENOA
(ITALY)

PORTORO
(ITALY)

GRANDE BRÈCHE
DE KLABER
(ALGERIA)

CANADIAN BLUE
(CANADA)

BARDIGLIO
FIORITO
(ITALY)

9. THE CHAPEL OF ST GEORGE AND THE ENGLISH MARTYRS

ARABESCATO
(ITALY)

ROSSO ANTICO
(GREECE)

BRÈCHE
SANGUINE
(ALGERIA)

SPANISH PINK
(SPAIN)

LAPIS LAZULI
(CHILE)

HOPTON
WOOD STONE
(ENGLAND)

PAVONAZZO
(ITALY)

SWEDISH
GREEN LIGHT
(SWEDEN)

NOIR BELGE
(BELGIUM)

RED GRIOTTE
(FRANCE)

10. THE CHAPEL OF ST JOSEPH

FIOR DI PESCO
(ITALY)

GREY
CANADIAN
ONYX
(CANADA)

VERDE ANTICO
PALE
(GREECE)

MEDICEA
BRECCIA
(ITALY)

HOPTON
WOOD STONE
(ENGLAND)

GREY
HYMETTIAN
(GREECE)

IRISH GREEN
(IRELAND)

YELLOW SIENA
(ITALY)

WHITE
CARRARA
(ITALY)

PURPLE
PORPHYRY
(EGYPT)

11. THE CHAPEL OF THE BLESSED SACRAMENT

CAMPAN VERT
(FRANCE)

ROSE DE
NUMIDIE
(ALGERIA)

CIPOLLINO
(GREECE)

VERDE ANTICO
DARK
(GREECE)

BRÈCHE
ORIENTALE
(FRANCE)

YELLOW SIENA
(ITALY)

RED
LANGUEDOC
(FRANCE)

GREEN
VARALLO
(ITALY)

12. THE SHRINE OF THE SACRED HEART AND ST MICHAEL

RED
LANGUEDOC
(FRANCE)

WHITE
CARRARA
(ITALY)

PAVONAZZO
(ITALY)

CAMPAN VERT
(FRANCE)

BLACK
PANDERMA
(TURKEY)

CIPOLLINO
(GREECE)

CARRARA
SECOND
STATUARY
(ITALY)

CORK RED
(IRELAND)

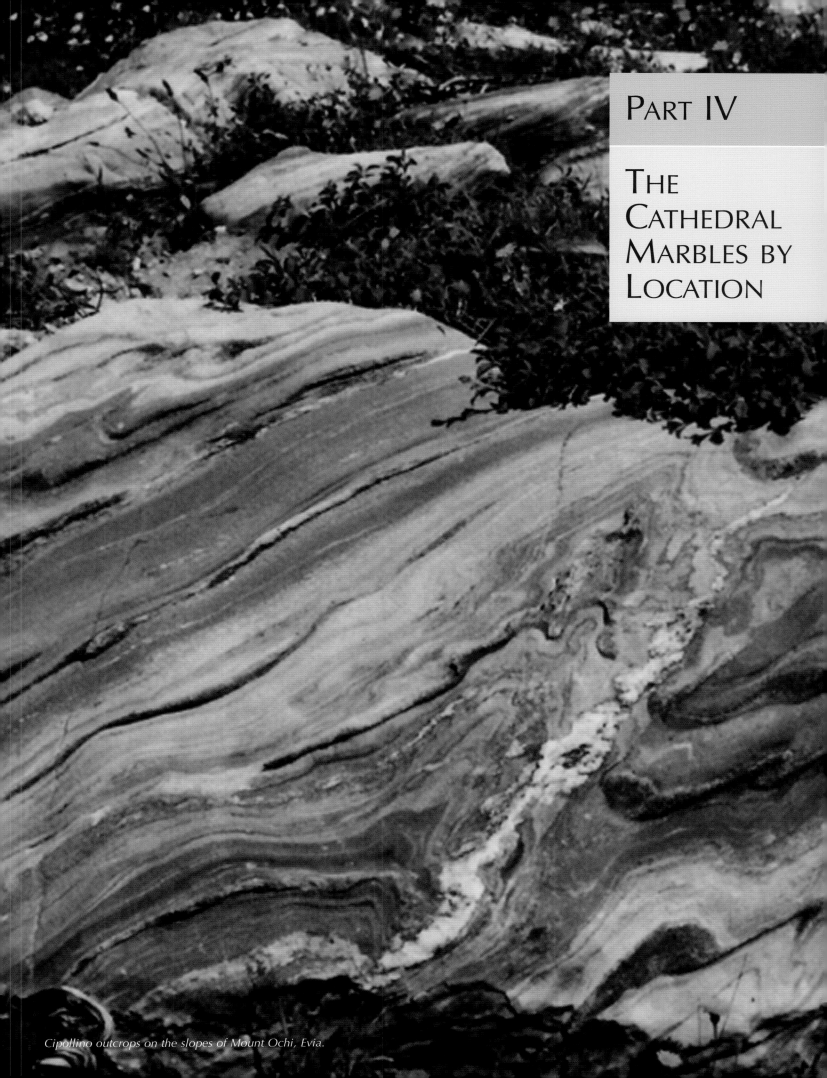

PART IV

THE
CATHEDRAL
MARBLES BY
LOCATION

Cipollino outcrops on the slopes of Mount Ochi, Evia.

NARTHEX AND NAVE

Marblework of nave and narthex floor 1903, organ gallery 1924, by Farmer & Brindley of 63 Westminster Bridge Road. Pulpit rebuilt 1934, nave piers clad 1947-9 and southwest corner of nave decorated 1956-7 by Fenning & Co of Rainville Road, Hammersmith. Nave arcades and galleries decorated 1959-63, narthex and porches 1963-4 by J Whitehead & Sons of Kennington Oval. Side porch plinths transferred 1963 from Church of the Assumption, Warwick Street. Numbers refer to Sources listed at end of Part VII.

SIDE PORCH WALLS

White Pentelic [4]
Verde Antico Pale [4]
Breccia Violetta [4]
Greek Cipollino [4]

MAIN PORCH WALLS AND FLOOR

White Pentelic
Greek Cipollino walls
Brèche Rose tympanum [16]
Belgian Grand Antique
Verde Antico

WEST ARCADE AND GALLERY
(Including organ screen 1924)

2nd Statuary [4]
Greek Cipollino [4]
Dark Derbyshire Fossil
Cork Red
Verde Antico Dark
Pavonazzo [4]
Roman Stone Light [4]
Seravezza Breccia [4]
Blue Hymettian [4]
Verde Antico Pale [4]
Rosso Antico [4]
Rosso Levanto [4]
Campan Vert
Purple Porphyry [4]
Giallo Antico [4]
Carrara Statuary capitals [1]
Imperial Red Granite columns [14,15]
Labradorite bases [1]

NARTHEX WALLS

2nd Statuary cornice
Breccia Violetta
Greek Cipollino
Derbyshire Fossil
Skyros [15,16]
Black/Grey Breccia (unidentified)
Cork Red
Brèche Sanguine disk [16]
Rosso Antico
Verde Antico Pale
Portoro skirting
Rosso Levanto

NAVE ARCADES AND GALLERIES
(Narthex to transepts)

2nd Statuary [5]
Yellow Siena (Gallery)
Cork Red [2]
Pavonazzo [5]
Greek Cipollino [5,19]
Breccia Violetta
Carrara Statuary capitals [1]
Verde Antico Dark columns [1,2,19]
Labradorite bases [1,2]
Brèche Sanguine (Gallery) [4]
Rosso Laguna (Gallery) [15,20]
Dark Derbyshire skirting
Campan Vert [5]
Azul Macaubas (Gallery) [15,20]
Rosso Levanto (Gallery)
Grand Antique des Pyrénées (Gallery)
Seravezza Breccia columns [16,19] b
Greek Cipollino columns [1,2,19]
Brèche du Nord (Gallery) [12]
Rosso Antico

NARTHEX FLOOR

2nd Statuary
Rosso Antico
Verde Antico [1]
Greek Cipollino
Yellow Siena
Bleu Fleuri [1] a

PLINTH (SIDE PORCHES)

Vert d'Estours [4]
Breccia Violetta

GIFT SHOP

Dark Shap columns [19]

NAVE FLOOR
(Below arcades)

2nd Statuary [1]
Belgian Grand Antique [1]
Greek Cipollino
Swedish Green (pulpit)
Verde Antico Dark (Heenan's tomb)

ST PETER'S STATUE

Carrara Statuary
Sicilian Onyx [15]
Grey Syenite [15]
Grand Antique des Pyrénées

PULPIT

2nd Statuary [5]
Pavonazzo [5,14]
Purple Porphyry [19]
Green Porphyry [19]
Greek Cipollino [5]

Note a: Source 1 lists these blue-grey paving slabs as Bleu Fleuri. Bardilla Bleu Fleuri is regarded by many as synonomous with Bardiglio Fiorito. See the Chapel of the Blessed Sacrament, Note a.

Note b: Both probably from near Seravezza, Tuscany. See Part VI, Note j.

NAVE AISLES AND TRANSEPTS

Marblework of aisle and transept floors 1903, south transept and passage to sacristy 1925-6, all by Farmer & Brindley of Westminster Bridge Road. Aisles 1930-1 and 1947-9, north transept 1947-9, passage north of sanctuary 1949, south of sanctuary 1953, all by Fenning & Co of Rainville Road, Hammersmith. Marblework above Vaughan Chantry and pierced screen above north transept 1949 by J Whitehead & Sons of Kennington Oval. Numbers refer to Sources listed at end of Part VII.

NORTH AISLE (From West)	SOUTH AISLE (From West)	TRANSEPTS (From West)
White Carrara cornice	White Carrara cornice [5]	Roman Stone Light [4]
Rosso Antico	Rosso Antico	Blue Hymettian [4]
Verde Antico Pale [5]	Greek Cipollino [5,19]	Pavonazzo [4]
Portoro skirting [5]	Dark/Light Derbyshire Fossil [5]	Rosso Antico [3]
Greek Cipollino [5]	Italian Cipollino [15]	Verde Antico Pale [4]
Dark Derbyshire Fossil [5]	Rosso Levanto	Dark Derbyshire Fossil [4]
Italian Cipollino [15]	Portoro skirting [5]	Greek Cipollino [4]
Bianco del Mare [5,19]	Verde Antico Pale	Yellow Siena *b*
Giallo Antico Light & Dark [5]	Campan Vert [5]	Campan Vert
Tortosa Broccatello [5,14,19]	Red Griotte [5] *a*	Rosso Levanto [4]
Dark Dove	Siena Breccia	Rouge Jaspé [3] *b*
Rosso Levanto [5]	Verde Corona [5]	Carrara Statuary capital
Siena Breccia	Arabescato [15]	Verde Antico column [1,2] *b*
Green/cream/black (unidentified)	Grey Hymettian	Labradorite base [1,2,4]
Arabescato [15]	Blue Hymettian [4]	Red Languedoc columns
Campan Vert [5]	Porfirico Rosso [5]	[1-4,19] *b*
Porfirico Rosso [5,15]	Pavonazzo [4]	
Pavonazzo		

NORTH AISLE FLOOR	SOUTH AISLE FLOOR	FLOOR OF TRANSEPTS
2nd Statuary [1]	2nd Statuary [1]	2nd Statuary [1]
Belgian Grand Antique [1]	Belgian Grand Antique [1]	
Greek Cipollino [1]	Greek Cipollino [1]	

Note a: Red Griotte is also on St George's Chapel floor. It seems to be Griotte d'Italie from Carcassonne in France (Sources 3, 4, 15, 19).

Note b: Yellow Siena, Rouge Jaspé and the Verde Antico column appear in the north transept only, the twin Red Languedoc columns in the south.

PASSAGES

NORTH OF SANCTUARY	SOUTH OF SANCTUARY	PASSAGE TO SACRISTY
2nd Statuary cornice	2nd Statuary cornice [5]	Pavonazzo
Rosso Levanto	Verde Issorie [5,15]	2nd Statuary
Verde Issorie [15]	Rosso Levanto [5]	Eretrian Red [13,15]
Dark Derbyshire Fossil	Nero Nube skirting [5,12]	Campan Vert
Red Languedoc [5]	Rose Phocéen [15]	Purple Porphyry
Campan Vert	Campan Vert	Verde Antico Pale
Rose Phocéen [15]	Red Languedoc [5]	Stazzema Breccia
Nero Nube skirting [5,12]	Dark Deryshire Fossil [5]	

SANCTUARY AND APSE

Marblework of tribunes and arcades 1902, St Edmund's shrine, Cardinal Manning's tomb 1907-10 all by J Whitehead & Sons of Kennington Oval. High altar 1902-3, baldacchino, altar steps and floor, sanctuary and apse screens 1905-6, apse wall 1921, all by Farmer & Brindley of Westminster Bridge Road. Numbers refer to Sources listed at end of Part VII.

TRIBUNES AND ARCADES

White Carrara [1,19]
Greek Cipollino
Red Verona [1,3,19]
Campan Vert [1,3,19]
Pavonazzo columns [1,3,4]
Rosso Levanto [1]
Breccia Violetta [19]
Verde Antico Dark [1,3,19]
Hopton Wood Stone [1,3]
Norwegian Pink columns [1-3,19]
Rouge Jaspé columns [1,3,19]
Derbyshire Fossil bases [1,19]

APSE WALL

2nd Statuary cornice [4]
Greek Cipollino [3,4]
Giallo Antico [4]
Noir Belge [4]
Rosso Antico [4]
Rose de Numidie [4]
Verde Antico Pale [3,4]

BALDACCHINO AND ALTAR

White Carrara [1,3,4]
Campan Vert [1,3]
Yellow Verona columns [1-3,19]
Verde Antico Pale [1,3,4,19]
Breccia Violetta [1,3]
Lapis Lazuli [1,4]
Purple Porphyry [1,3,4,]
Cornish granite altar [1-3,19]

ARCHBISHOP'S THRONE 1902

Carrara, Rosso Antico [15]
Verde Ranocchia [12]
Onyx, Breccia di Arbe [13]

APSE SCREEN

2nd Statuary [1]
Greek Cipollino [1,3]
Giallo Antico
Rouge Antique [1,14]

APSE BALCONIES

Cipollino Dorato columns [18]

ALTAR STEPS AND FLOOR

Derbyshire Fossil [5]
Giallo Antico [1]
Yellow Siena [1]
Red Languedoc [1]
Campan Vert [1]
2nd Statuary steps [1]
Verde Antico Dark [1]
Rosso Antico [1,19]
Cork Red [1]

SANCTUARY SCREEN

Rosso Antico [1,2,19]
2nd Statuary frames [1]
Siena Breccia [13,15]

SACRISTY

Labradorite column

ST PETER'S CRYPT

ST EDMUND'S SHRINE

Repen Zola arch
Cork Red
Rosso Antico
Hopton Wood Stone
Swedish Green Dark [15,16]

INNER CRYPT FLOOR

Grey Bardiglio [15]
Hopton Wood Stone
Rosso Levanto [15]
Greek Cipollino [1]

CARDINAL WISEMAN'S TOMB

White Statuary
Cork Red
Alabaster [1,15]
Rosso Levanto Antico [15]

MAIN CRYPT

Imperial Red granite (screen and far columns) [12,15]
Dark Shap red granite (near columns) [12,15]
Carmen Red granite (middle columns) [12,15]
Greek Cipollino (wall cladding) [1,3,5]
Hopton Wood Stone [1,3,5]

CARDINAL MANNING'S TOMB

Repen Zola arch [8]
Cork Red
Greek Cipollino [1,3]
Rosso Antico [4]
Campan Mélangé [1]

THE BAPTISTRY

Marblework of Baptistry screen 1902-3, walls 1969 by J Whitehead & Sons of Kennington Oval. Font made in Rome 1901, installed 1902. Floor 1912 by Farmer & Brindley of Westminster Bridge Road. Numbers refer to Sources listed at end of Part VII.

BAPTISTRY SCREEN

White Carrara [1,3]
Campan Vert [1,3,15,16,22]
Verde Antico Pale
Portoro skirting [1,3]
Violet Breccia [1,3]
Campan Rouge [15,16,22]
Campan Rose et Vert [15,16,22]
Pavonazzo columns [1,3,19] *a*

BAPTISMAL FONT

Pavonazzo [1,3,19]
Verde Antico Pale [1,3,19]
Verde Olivo [16]
Cipollino [1,3]
Rosso Antico [8]
White Statuary

OTHER WALLS

White Carrara
Greek Cipollino
Dark Derbyshire Fossil
Pavonazzo
Violet Breccia

FLOOR AND FONT STEPS

Carrara 2nd Statuary
Verde Antico Pale [19]
Greek Cipollino [19]
Yellow Siena [1,3,16,19]
Connemara Green [1,19]
Giallo Antico [1]
Rosso Antico [1,19]

Note a: Source 1 lists these columns as Greek. See Part VI, Note *h*.

CHAPEL OF ST GREGORY AND ST AUGUSTINE

Marblework 1902-4 by J Whitehead & Sons of Kennington Oval. For Baptistry screen marbles see above.

EAST WALL AND ALTAR

White Carrara [1]
Campan Vert [1,3,5,19]
Verde Antico Pale [3]
Portoro skirting
Rosso Levanto [5]
Campan Rouge [2,15,16,22]
Rouge Jaspé [1-3,5,19]
Swiss Cipollino [1-3]
Greek Cipollino [1-3,19]
Pavonazzo [1,3]
Norwegian Pink [1-3,19]
Lapis Lazuli [1,3,5,19]
Yellow Siena frontal [1-3,5,19]

OTHER WALLS

White Carrara [1]
Light Breccia [1-3] *b*
Rosso Levanto [1,3,5,19]
Portoro skirting [5]
Verde di Mare panel [5]
Swiss Cipollino panel
Verde Antico Pale [1,3,19]
Campan Vert [1,2,5,19]
Campan Mélangé [1]
Pink Verona [15,16] *c*
Red Verona [15,16] *c*
Carrara Statuary capitals [1]
Swiss Cipollino columns [1,2,19]
Labradorite base [1]

ALTAR STEPS AND FLOOR
Labradorite
Hopton Wood Stone
Vein Statuary steps [5]
Brèche Violette [1,5]
Bardiglio Fiorito [1,3]
Noir Belge [16]
Verde Cesana [16]
Yellow Siena [1,5,16]
Red Broccatello [1,3,19] *c*
Acqua Bianca [16]

Note b: In a drawing Bentley lists this as 'Breccia Peterocchia'. It is clearly Tuscan and appears to be a breccia from the Stazzema area.

Note c: Sources 1 and 3 list the arch soffit marbles as pink Verona and light red Broccatello. They also list the orange predella panel as Broccatello. These marbles are varieties of Pink Verona (Rosato Verona) or Red Verona (Rosso Verona).

CHAPEL OF ST PATRICK AND THE SAINTS OF IRELAND

Marblework of altar 1910, walls and floor 1923-8, aisle screen 1929-30 by Farmer & Brindley of Westminster Bridge Road. Reredos 1961 by J Whitehead & Sons. Numbers refer to Sources listed at end of Part VII.

EAST WALL AND ALTAR

2nd Statuary cornice [5]
Verde Alpi [5,15]
Campan Vert [5]
Verde Corona [5]
Red Languedoc [4,5,19]
Lapis Lazuli [4,5,19]
Africano [5,13,19]
Pavonazzo [3-5,19]
Verde Antico Pale [3,4,19]
Green Tinos [15]
White Carrara canopy [4]
Emperor's Red [19]
Yellow Verona columns [3,4,19]
Italian Cipollino [1,3,5]
Irish Green Fossil [1] a
Skyros Breccia [13,17]
Green Smaragdite
Irish Black Fossil [1-3,19]
Connemara Green [1-3]
Victoria Red [1-3] b
Purple Porphyry [4,5]

OTHER WALLS

2nd Statuary [2]
Rosso Levanto
Breccia Violetta [15]
Cork Red colonnettes [19]
Verde Antico Pale [19]
Jaune de Var [15,19]
Purple Porphyry [2-4,19]
Pavonazzo
Swedish Green [4,19]
Blue Hymettian strips
Vert d'Estours [4,19]
Green Smaragdite [2-4,19]
Brèche Universelle [2-4,19] c
Campan Vert
Carrara Statuary capital
Greek Cipollino column [1]
Laboradorite base [1]

ALTAR STEPS AND FLOOR

2nd Statuary steps [5]
Labradorite
Yellow Siena [3,5,19]
Connemara Green [3-5,19]
Irish Black [4,5]
Cork Red [3-5,19]
Vert d'Estours [3,5,19]
Irish Green Light [5] a
Green Verdite [5,12,14]
Lapis Lazuli [3,5]
Amazon Green [3,5]
Rosso Antico [5]

Note a: Connemara Green from Streamstown quarry near Clifden, as on the altar and floor. Irish Green Light possibly from Barnanoraun quarry north of Ballynahinch.

Note b: A particularly attractive form of deep red Cork Red marble from Ireland in which crinoid rings are clearly visible.

Note c: For Brèche Universelle, here and in the Lady Chapel, see Part VI, Note e.

CHAPEL OF ST ANDREW AND THE SAINTS OF SCOTLAND

Marblework 1913-15 by Farmer & Brindley of Westminster Bridge Road.

EAST WALL AND ALTAR

Rosso Antico [1]
White Pentelic [1,3]
Giallo Antico
Cipollino [1]
Blue Hymettian [1,2]
Verde Antico Pale [1,3,19]
Greek Cipollino [1]
Purple Porphyry [1,3]
Alloa Granite [1,3,19]
Peterhead Granite [1,3,19]
Aberdeen Granite [1,3,19]

OTHER WALLS

White Pentelic [1,3]
Giallo Antico [1,3]
Blue Hymettian [1,2,19]
Pavonazzo [1,3]
Rosso Levanto [1,3]
Greek Cipollino [1,3]
Rosso Collemandina columns [16]
Old Cipollino [1,19]
Red Skyros [1-3,19]
Rosso Antico
Carrara Statuary capital [1]
Swiss Cipollino column [1]
Labradorite base

CHAPEL OF ST PAUL

Marblework 1913-17 by Farmer & Brindley of Westminster Bridge Road. Altar 1910 by J Whitehead & Sons of Kennington Oval. Floor 1940 by Fenning & Co of Rainville Road, Hammersmith. Numbers refer to Sources listed at end of Part VII.

EAST WALL AND ALTAR

White Carrara cornice
Grey Hymettian [19]
Greek Cipollino [3,4,19]
Campan Vert [3-5,19]
Rosso Levanto [5]
Proconnesian [3,4,19]
Hopton Wood Stone [5]
Verde Antico Pale [5]
Pavonazzo [1,19]
2nd Statuary altar [1]
Purple Porphyry [3,8,19] *a*
Green Tinos [1-4,19]

OTHER WALLS

White Carrara cornice
Grey Hymettian [3,4,19]
Greek Cipollino [1,3,4,19]
Verde Antico Pale [1,3,4]
Italian Cipollino
Cipollino Rosso [13,14]
Pavonazzo columns [1,3,4,19]
Bardiglietto column [4,5,12]
Statuary frames [1]
Rosso Levanto
Swedish Green Light [15]
Carrara Statuary capital [1]
Greek Cipollino column [1,4]
Labradorite base

ALTAR STEPS AND FLOOR

Labradorite
White Pentelic [3-5]
Verde Antico Dark [3]
Purple Porphyry [3,4]
Green Porphyry [3,4]
Verde Antico Pale [3,4]

Note a: The altar frontal side panels were listed incorrectly as Rosso Antico by Sources 1 and 2 but as Purple Porphyry by Sources 3, 8, 19.

THE LADY CHAPEL

Marblework 1908 by Farmer & Brindley of Westminster Bridge Road. Nave floor 1956 by Fenning & Co of Rainville Road, Hammersmith.

APSE AND ALTAR

White Carrara [1-3]
Campan Vert [1,3,19]
Rosso Antico [1,3,4]
Grey Irish Fossil [1,3]
Pavonazzo [1,3]
Pink Pavonazzo [1-4,14,19]
Numidian Red [5] *b*
Grand Antique des Pyrénées [1]
Golden Italian Breccia [1] *c*
Purple Breccia [1,3,4]
Irish Green [5,15]
Purple Veined Siena [1,3] *c*
Lapis Lazuli [1]
Greek Cipollino [1,3,4]

OTHER WALLS

White Carrara [1-3]
Irish Green [5,15]
Purple Breccia [1,3,4]
Giallo Antico [1-4,19]
Campan Vert [1,3,19]
Pavonazzo [1,3,19]
Verde Antico Pale [1,3,4,19]
Rosso Antico [1,3,4]
Irish Grey Fossil [1,3]
Stazzema Breccia [16]

ALTAR STEPS AND FLOOR

2nd Statuary [1]
Noir Belge [1]
Yellow Siena *c*
Cork Red
Verde Antico Pale [1-3]
Green Tinos [15]
Greek Cipollino
Red Languedoc [1,3]
Purple Veined Siena [1,3] *c*
Grey Greek marble [1,3]
(unidentified)
Brèche Universelle [2,4]
Connemara Green [15]
Rosso Antico [15]

Note b: Numidian Red is Brèche Sanguine from Kleber, Algeria. Here it refers to the decorative diamonds above the apse doors. Source 5 also used the name for the small panels above the Chief Pastors in the north aisle.

Note c: The beautiful veined yellow panel above the altar, inset with green Campan Vert and listed as Purple Veined Siena by Sources 1 and 3, could be Giallo Dorato Antico from Chemtou, Tunisia, according to Source 13. The other examples of Siena marble in the chapel are all common examples of Yellow Siena.

CHAPEL OF THE HOLY SOULS

Marblework 1902, floor 1906 by J Whitehead & Sons of Kennington Oval. Numbers refer to Sources listed at end of Part VII.

EAST WALL AND ALTAR	OTHER WALLS	ALTAR STEPS AND FLOOR
White Carrara	Fawn Repen Zola [1-3]	Bardiglio Fiorito [1-3]
Dark Dove [1] *a*	Carrara Statuary capital [2]	Rosso Antico, *b*
Rosso Levanto [2,3,19]	Labradorite column [1-3,19]	Swedish Green Dark [15]
Portoro skirting [4]	Dark Dove [1] *a*	Noir Belge
Noir Belge [1-3]	Rosso Levanto [1,3,5,19]	Grande Brèche de Klaber [1]
Brèche Verte [1-3]	Portoro skirting [4]	Canadian Blue [1-3]
Bardiglio Fiorito [1-3]	Green Genoa [5,19]	Yellow Siena [1-3]
Vert des Alpes [5,15]	Bardiglio Fiorito [1-3,5,19]	Labradorite
Green Genoa [1-3,19]	Verde di Mare [1,2]	
Brèche Violette [5]	Imperial Yellow [1] *c*	**GERONTIUS PANELS**
Greek Cipollino [1-3]	Pavonazzo column [1-3,5]	
Portoro frontal [1-3,19]	Green Tinos [1-3]	Canadian Blue, Lido,
		Rosso Levanto,
		Crema di Valencia,
		Verde di Mare,
		Carrara, Swedish Green,
		Yellow Siena,
		Brèche de Kleber (All Source 16).

Note a: Dark Dove is a dark grey Italian marble from the Versilia area of Tuscany in Italy and resembles Bardiglio Capella (Sources 12, 15, 21).

Note b: The original predella panel of French Rouge Antique installed by J Whitehead & Sons in 1906 was replaced by Farmer & Brindley with a panel of Rosso Antico in 1927.

Note c: Imperial Yellow is a form of Portoro (Source 12).

CHAPEL OF ST GEORGE AND THE ENGLISH MARTYRS

Marblework of altar 1910 by Arthur Lee & Bros of Hayes, Middlesex. Floor 1930, altarpiece surround 1947-9, by Fenning & Co of Rainville Road, Hammersmith. Walls 1949 by J Whitehead & Sons of Kennington Oval. Altarpiece 1939-40 by Eric Gill, installed 1946.

EAST WALL AND ALTAR	OTHER WALLS	ALTAR STEPS AND FLOOR
White Carrara cornice	Carrara Statuary capital [1]	White Pentelic [3,5,19]
Arabescato [15,21]	Swiss Cipollino column [1-3,19]	Spanish Pink [3-5,12,19] *f*
Greek Cipollino	Labradorite base [1,3]	Red Griotte [3-5,15,19]
Pavonazzo [1,3,5,19] *d*	Arabescato [15,21]	Noir Belge [3-5,19]
Rosso Antico [2,3,5,19]	Greek Cipollino	Lapis Lazuli [2,4,5,19]
Swedish Green Light	Pavonazzo [5]	Amazon Green [5,19]
Hopton Wood Stone [3,4]	Rosso Antico	Arabescato [15,21]
Verde Antico Pale [1,3,19]	Swedish Green Light [5,15]	
Brèche Sanguine [3,5,19] *e*	Hopton Wood Stone	
	(St George) [19]	

Note d: Wall panels from Seravezza, columns from Carrara. See Part VI, Note *h*.

Note e: Listed as Rouge Sanguine from Klaber by Source 1. Similar to the Holy Souls floor panel listed by Source 1 as Grande Brèche de Klaber.

Note f: Spanish Pink appears to be Rosa Valencia (Marmor Rosa) from Jativa Quarries, Barxeta in Buscarro, Valencia (Sources 12, 16).

CHAPEL OF ST JOSEPH

Marblework of altar 1910, apse 1914, by Farmer & Brindley of Westminster Bridge Road. Walls 1934-5 and 1939, floor 1939, by Fenning & Co of Rainville Road, Hammersmith. Numbers refer to Sources listed at end of Part VII.

EAST WALL AND ALTAR	OTHER WALLS	ALTAR STEPS AND FLOOR
White Carrara cornice	Carrara Statuary capital [1]	White Carrara steps [3,19]
Medicea Breccia [15] a	Greek Cipollino column [1-5]	Hopton Wood Stone [2-4]
Greek Cipollino [3,4]	Labradorite base	Purple Porphyry [2-4]
Grey Hymettian, b	Medicea Breccia [15] a	Green Porphyry [2-4]
Rosso Antico [3]	Fior di Pesco [2-5,14,15]	Rosso Antico [3,4]
Verde Antico Pale [3]	Canadian Grey Onyx [4,5]	Brèche Universelle [3,4]
Pavonazzo [1,3,19]	Bianco del Mare arches [5,19]	Dark Derbyshire Fossil
Lapis Lazuli [1,3,8,19]	Breccia Oniciata columns [15,16] d	
Yellow Siena [1-3,19]	Verde Antico Pale [2,5]	
Irish Green [1-3,19] c	Fior di Pesco column [2-5,14,15]	

Note a: Source 16 identifies these wall panels as Breccia Verde (Brèche Verte) di Seravezza. Both Breccia Verde and Breccia Medicea are quarried at Mulina close to Stazzema and 3-4 miles from Seravezza in the Apuan Alps.

Note b: Only Source 3 lists this apse wall marble, and then simply as white Greek marble. It appears identical to the soft grey marble on the walls of St Paul's Chapel which is listed as Greek Hymettian.

Note c: This green marble appears to be a particularly attractive variety of Connemara Green from Lissoughter quarry near Recess in County Galway.

Note d: Sources 3 and 5 list these eight beige and white colonnettes below the windows as Ibex Agate, Source 4 as Hiberian Agate. Both Sources 15 and 16 believe this marble to be a form of Breccia Oniciata from the Nuvolento area of Lombardy, Italy. It seems likely to be the variety known as Breccia Damascata.

CHAPEL OF ST THOMAS OF CANTERBURY – THE VAUGHAN CHANTRY

Marblework 1907-10 by Farmer & Brindley of Westminster Bridge Road.

EAST WALL AND ALTAR	OTHER WALLS	ALTAR STEPS AND FLOOR
White Statuary	Verde Antico Pale [1,3]	White Carrara steps
Rosso Antico	Carrara Statuary capital [1,3]	Irish Green [1,3,5] e
Pavonazzo [1,3]	Grd Ant des Pyrénées column	Rosso Antico [3]
Verde Antico Pale [1,3,4,19]	[1-3,19]	Yellow Siena [3,5]
Dark Derbyshire Fossil	Rosso Antico [1,3]	Bardiglio Fiorito
	Pavonazzzo [1,3]	
	White Pentelic effigy [1,3,19]	
	Verde Antico Dark base [19]	

Note e: Another Connemara Green marble, this time possibly from Barnanoraun quarry, six miles east of Clifden and north of Ballynahinch in County Galway.

CHAPEL OF THE BLESSED SACRAMENT

Marblework 1904-7 by Farmer & Brindley of Westminster Bridge Road. Numbers refer to Sources listed at end of Part VII.

APSE AND ALTAR

White Carrara cornice [1]
Campan Vert [1,3]
Rose de Numidie [1-3,8]
Pavonazzo [1-3,19]
Brèche Orientale [15]
Yellow Siena [1-3]
Greek Cipollino [1-3]
Verde Antico Pale [1-3]
Red Languedoc altar [2]
Lapis Lazuli [1]

OTHER WALLS

White Carrara cornice [1]
Verde Antico Pale [1-3,19]
Dark Siena [1-3,19]
Campan Vert [1-3,19]
Brèche Orientale [15]
Bardiglio Fiorito [2,3] *a*
Rose de Numidie [1-3,8,19]
Pavonazzo [1-3,19]

ALTAR STEPS AND FLOOR

White Carrara steps [1]
Greek Cipollino [1,2]
Red Languedoc [1-3]
Verde Antico [1,2]
Yellow Siena [1,2]
Green Varallo [1]
Bardiglio Fiorito [2] *a*
Rosso Antico
Cork Red

Note a: Sources 2 and 3 list the mottled blue-grey marble supporting the bronze screens on either side of the chapel nave as grey Bardiglio. Source 1 lists the blue-grey hexagonal slabs on the floor in front of the chapel as Bleu Fleuri, Source 2 as Bardiglio. Most authorities take Bardiglio Fiorito and Bardilla Bleu Fleuri to be synonomous but some take the latter to be a lighter, more flowery variety (as below the screens). They are quarried in the Versilia, Massa and Carrara areas of Tuscany in Italy.

SHRINE OF THE SACRED HEART AND ST MICHAEL

Marblework 1910 by Farmer & Brindley of Westminster Bridge Road.

APSE AND ALTAR

White Carrara cornice [1]
Greek Cipollino [1,5]
Pavonazzo [1,5]
Campan Vert [1,5]
Red Languedoc [1,5]
Cork Red altar [1,5]
Black Panderma [1,20]
White marble statue [1] *b*
2nd Statuary (St Michael) [1]

OTHER WALLS

White Carrara [1,5]
Verde Antico Pale [1] *c*
Greek Cipollino [1,5]
Irish Black skirting [15]
Stazzema Breccia [16]
Rosso Antico [1,20]
Pavonazzo [1,5]

ALTAR STEPS AND FLOOR

Labradorite
Grey Fossil
Red Languedoc

Note b: Source 1 describes this as white marble and also as alabaster.

Note c: Source 1 describes the vertical bands below the windows on the north wall as Pavonazzo and Irish fossil marble. The latter, however, is Verde Antico from Greece.

METHODOLOGY AND SOURCES

In these tables the marbles in each chapel or other location are listed downwards from the top left of each wall (or floor) before moving to the immediate right and repeating the process. Each marble only appears once in each list except in the case of main columns . Numbers refer to the Sources used to identify each marble and are listed at the end of Part VII.

The Verde Antico quarries with the quarrymen's church in the distance.

PART V – EXAMPLES AND ORIGINS

Letters refer to Notes in Part VI. Numbers refer to Sources listed at the end of Part VII.

MARBLE	COLOUR	EXAMPLE	ORIGIN
Aberdeen Granite [1,19]	Speckled grey	Altar base, St Andrew's Chapel	Aberdeen, Scotland
Acqua Bianca [16]	Clear white	Cardinal Hume's tomb	Carrara, Italy
Africano [5,13,19]	Cloudy grey/red	E. wall niches, St Patrick's Chapel	Sigacik, Turkey
Alabaster [4,20]	Pink & white	Our Lady's statue	Chellaston, England
Alloa Granite [1,3,19]	Speckled grey	Altar top, St Andrew's Chapel	Alloa, Scotland
Amazon Green [3,5]	Turquoise	Predella, St Patrick's Chapel	Colorado, USA
Arabescato [15,21]	Veined white	Walls and Floor, St George's Chapel	Versilia, Italy
Azul Macaubas [15,20]	Pale blue	Nave gallery panels	Macaubas, Brazil
Bardiglietto [4,5,12]	Grey/blue/white	S. wall column, St Paul's Chapel	Massa, Italy
Grey Bardiglio [15]	Blue-grey	Altar steps, St Edmund's Shrine	Massa, Italy
Bardiglio Fiorito [1-3]	Dark veined grey	Floor, Holy Souls Chapel	Versilia, Italy
Belgian Grand Antique [1]	Black & white	Nave floor	Hainault, Belgium
Bianco del Mare [5,19] b	Light buff	N. wall arch, St Joseph's Chapel	Split, Yugoslavia
Breccia di Arbe [13]	Speckled sand	Archbishop's throne	Arbe, Yugoslavia
Breccia Oniciata [15,16]	Beige and white	N. wall columns, St Joseph's Chapel	Nuvolento, Italy
Breccia Violetta [4] c	Purple & white	Side porch walls	Seravezza, Italy
Brèche du Nord [12]	Grey breccia	Nave gallery panels	Namur, Belgium
Brèche Orientale [15]	Dark breccia	Arch soffits, Blessed Sacrament Chapel	Baixas, France
Brèche Rose [16] d	Orange breccia	Entrance tympanum	Kleber, Algeria
Brèche Sanguine [4] d	Red breccia	Nave gallery panels	Kleber, Algeria
Brèche Universelle [2,4] e	Green conglomerate	Floor, Lady Chapel	Hammamat, Egypt
Brèche Verte [1-3]	Cream/black/green	Niches, Holy Souls Chapel	Stazzema, Italy
Campan Mélangé [1]	Red/white/green	W. wall, Ss Gregory & Augustine's Chapel	Campan, France
Campan Rose et Vert [15]	Pinkish green	Baptistry screen	Campan, France
Campan Rouge [15,16,22]	Red & white	E. wall, Ss Gregory & Augustine's Chapel	Campan, France
Campan Vert [1,3,5,19]	Mottled green	E. wall, Ss Gregory & Augustine's Chapel	Campan, France
Canadian Blue [1-3]	Dark blue	Floor, Holy Souls Chapel	Bancroft, Canada
Canadian Grey Onyx [4,5]	Blue-grey	N. wall, St Joseph's Chapel	Bancroft, Canada
Carmen Red Granite [12] f	Pink & black	Middle columns, Crypt	Kotka, Finland
Carrara Statuary [1]	Plain white	Column capitals	Carrara, Italy
Carrara 2nd Statuary [1]	Veined white	Paving, Nave	Carrara, Italy
White Carrara [5]	Plain white	Aisle cornices	Carrara, Italy
Cipollino Dorato [18]	Yellow & black	Apse balcony columns	Valdieri, Italy
Cipollino Rosso [13,14]	White banded red	S. wall, St Paul's Chapel	Iasos, Turkey
Connemara Green [3-5]	Wavy dark green	Floor slabs, St Patrick's Chapel	Clifden, Ireland
Cork Red [3-5,19]	Mottled red	Colonnettes, St Patrick's Chapel	Baneshane, Ireland
Cornish Granite [1-3,19]	Speckled grey	High altar	Penryn, England
Crema Valencia [16]	Pink-flushed Cream	Gerontius panel, Holy Souls Chapel	Valencia, Spain
Derbyshire Fossil [5]	Grey or brown	Aisle skirting	Wirksworth, England
Dark Dove [1]	Mid grey	Wall corners, Holy Souls Chapel	Versilia, Italy
Emperor's Red [19]	Orange red	Above altar, St Patrick's Chapel	Lisbon, Portugal
Eretrian Red [13,15]	Red & white	Passage to Sacristy	Eretria, Greece
Fantastico Viola [15]	Swirling purple	Floor, St Andrew's Chapel	Seravezza, Italy
Fior di Pesco [2-5,14,15]	Purple & white	N. wall column, St Joseph's Chapel	Stazzema, Italy
Green Genoa [5,19]	Veined dark green	West wall, Holy Souls Chapel	Genoa, Italy
Giallo Antico [1-4,19] d	Pink-yellow	Walls, Lady Chapel	Kleber, Algeria
Giallo Antico [4] d	Yellow-brown	Cross, organ loft	Chemtou, Tunisia
Gr. Ant. Pyrénées [1-3,19]	Black & white	Columns, St Thomas Becket Chapel	Aubert, France
Gr. Brèche de Klaber [1] d	Blood red	Floor, Holy Souls Chapel	Kleber, Algeria

Greek Cipollino [1-5]	Wavy green	Entrance column, St Joseph's Chapel	Evia, Greece
Red Griotte [3-5,15,19]	Dark cherry red	Floor, St George's Chapel	Carcassonne, France
Hopton Wood [2-4] b	Grey limestone	Floor, St Joseph's Chapel	Wirksworth, England
Blue Hymettian [1,2,19]	Soft blue-grey	Walls, St Andrew's Chapel	Hymettus, Greece
Grey Hymettian [3,4,19]	Soft blue-grey	Walls, St Paul's Chapel	Hymettus, Greece
Imperial Red [12,15] f	Red granite	Columns, Narthex	Kalmar, Sweden
Imperial Yellow [1]	Black & yellow	N. wall, Holy Souls Chapel	Portovenere, Italy
Iona Green [1,3,19]	Pale sea green	Floor, St Andrew's Chapel	Iona, Scotland
Irish Black [4,5]	Grey-black	Floor, St Patrick's Chapel	Kilkenny, Ireland
Irish Black Fossil [1-3,19]	Black fossil	Altar, St Patrick's Chapel	Kilkenny, Ireland
Irish Green [1,3,19]	Wavy green	Altar, St Joseph's Chapel	Recess, Ireland
Irish Grey Fossil [1,3]	Grey fossil	Niches, Lady Chapel	Co Offaly, Ireland
Italian Cipollino [1,3,5]	Green & white	Altar, St Patrick's Chapel	Versilia, Italy
Jaune de Var [15,19]	Mottled yellow	S. wall column, St Patrick's Chapel	Brignoles, France
Labradorite [1,3] g	Grey-black	Nave column bases	Larvik, Norway
Red Languedoc [1-4,19]	Rose & white	Twin columns, Lady Chapel	Caunes, France
Lapis Lazuli [4,5,19]	Dark blue	Niches, St Patrick's Chapel	Ovalle, Chile
Lido [16]	Grey	Gerontius panel, Holy Souls Chapel	Tiflet, Morocco
Medicea Breccia [15]	Cream & black	W. wall, St Joseph's Chapel	Seravezza, Italy
Nero Nube [5,12]	Grey fossil	Passage skirting	Lombardy, Italy
Noir Belge [1-3]	Plain black	Niches, Holy Souls Chapel	Namur, Belgium
Norwegian Pink [1-3,19]	Pale pink	Altar, Ss Gregory & Augustine's Chapel	Fauske, Norway
Panderma [1,20]	Streaked black	Apse wall, Sacred Heart Shrine	Bandirma, Turkey
Pavonazzo [1,3,4] h	Purple & cream	Tribune columns	Seravezza, Italy
Pavonazzo [1-4,14,19] h	Pink on cream	Apse walls, Lady Chapel	Seravezza, Italy
Pavonazzo [5,11,14] h	Grey/green vein	Pulpit	Carrara, Italy
Pavonazzo [1,3,4,11,19] h	Blue vein	S. wall columns, St Paul's Chapel	Carrara, Italy
White Pentelic [1,3]	Plain white	Baldacchino, St Andrew's Chapel	Pentelicon, Greece
Peterhead Granite [1,3,19]	Speckled red	Altar columns, St Andrew's Chapel	Peterhead, Scotland
Porfirico Rosso [5,15]	Speckled dark red	End of north aisle	Trento, Italy
Green Porphyry [3,4]	Speckled green	Floor, St Paul's Chapel	Stephania, Greece
Purple Porphyry [3,4]	Speckled dark red	Floor, St Paul's Chapel	Gebel Dokhan, Egypt
Portoro [1-3,19]	Black & yellow	Altar frontal, Holy Souls Chapel	Portovenere, Italy
Proconnesian [3,4,19]	White & grey	Apse wall, St Paul's Chapel	Marmara, Turkey
Repen Zola [1-3] b	Speckled buff	Arch soffits, Holy Souls Chapel	Istria, Yugoslavia
Roman Stone [4,8] b	Light buff	Organ loft arches	Istria, Yugoslavia
Rose de Numidie [1-3,8] d	Pink on yellow	Piers, Blessed Sacrament Chapel	Kleber, Algeria
Rose Phocéen [15]	Bright red	N & S Sanctuary Passages	Toulon, France
Rosso Antico [1,12,19]	Dark red	Sanctuary screen	The Mani, Greece
Rosso Collemandina [16]	Dark red	S. wall columns, St Andrew's Chapel	Garfagnana, Italy
Rosso Laguna [15,20] i	Dark red	Nave gallery panels	Becin Kale, Turkey
Rosso Levanto [1,3,5]	Dark broken red	Wall seat, Ss Gregory & Augustine's Chapel	La Spezia, Italy
Rouge Antique [1,14]	Dark red	Apse screen, Sanctuary	Cessenon, France
Rouge Jaspé [1,3,19]	Yellowish red	Side columns, Sanctuary	Vitrolles, France
Seravezza Breccia [4] c, j	Purple & cream	Organ loft columns	Seravezza, Italy
Dark Shap [12,15,19] f	Pink granite	Shop & near columns in Crypt	Cumbria, England
Sicilian Onyx [15]	Yellow-brown	Plinth of St Peter's statue	Sicily, Italy
Siena Breccia [13,15]	Black & yellow	Sanctuary screen	Siena, Italy
Purple Veined Siena [1] k	Veined yellow	Predella, Lady Chapel	Siena, Italy
Yellow Siena [1,3,5,19] k	Deep yellow	Altar, Ss Gregory & Augustine's Chapel	Siena, Italy
Skyros [1-3,19]	Red & yellow	W. wall, St Andrew's Chapel	Skyros, Greece
Smaragdite [2-4,19]	Bright green	W. wall, St Patrick's Chapel	Corsica, France
Spanish Pink [3-5,12,19]	Veined pink	Floor, St George's Chapel	Valencia, Spain

Stazzema Breccia [16]	Dark breccia	Wall panels, Sacred Heart Shrine	Stazzema, Italy
Swedish Green Dark [15]	Grey-green	Floor, Holy Souls Chapel	Norrkoping, Sweden
Swedish Green Light [5,15]	Pale green	Walls, St George's Chapel	Norrkoping, Sweden
Swiss Cipollino [1,2,19]	Yellow green	N. cols, Ss Gregory & Augustine's Chapel	Saillon, Switzerland
Grey Syenite [15]	Speckled grey	St Peter's plinth	Piedmont, Italy
Green Tinos [1-4,19]	Mottled green	Frontal, St Paul's Chapel	Tinos, Greece
Tortosa Broccatello [5,14]	Red & yellow	Below list of Chief Pastors, N. aisle	Tarragona, Spain
Green Varallo [1]	Veined green	Floor panels, Blessed Sacrament Chapel	Piedmont, Italy
Verde Alpi [5,15]	Veined dark green	E. wall, St Patrick's Chapel	Piedmont, Italy
Verde Antico Dark [1,19]	Green & black	8 columns, Nave	Larissa, Greece
Verde Antico Pale [19]	Green & black	S. wall, St Patrick's Chapel	Larissa, Greece
Verde Cesana [16]	Dark green	Floor, Ss Gregory & Augustine's Chapel	Piedmont, Italy
Verde Corona [5]	Moss green	E. wall, St Patrick's Chapel	Val d'Aosta, Italy
Verde di Mare [1,2]	Swirling dark green	N. wall, Holy Souls Chapel	Genoa, Italy
Verde Issorie [5,15]	Veined green	N & S Sanctuary Passages	Val d'Aosta, Italy
Verde Olivo [16]	Moss green	Font, Baptistry	Val d'Aosta, Italy
Verde Ranocchia [12,13]	Green & yellow	Archbishop's throne	Wadi Atalia, Egypt
Verdite [5,12,14]	Light or dark green	Floor, St Patrick's Chapel	Barberton, South Africa
Pink Verona [15,16] /	Pink-fawn	Soffits, Ss Gregory & Augustine's Chapel	Verona, Italy
Red Verona [1,3,19] /	Mottled orange	Tribune panels	Verona, Italy
Yellow Verona [1,3,19] /	Deep yellow	Baldacchino columns	Verona, Italy
Vert des Alpes [5,15]	Veined dark green	Beside altar, Holy Souls Chapel	Cottian, France
Vert d'Estours [4]	Green & white	Side porch plinths	Ariège, France
Victoria Red [1-3]	Deep red	Altar front, St Patrick's Chapel	Baneshane, Ireland

Alternative Names

Dark Dove. Resembles Bardiglio Capella from Versilia, Lucca, Tuscany. [12,15,21]
Emperor's Red. Encarnado from near Lisbon, Portugal. [6,8]
Imperial Yellow. Portoro from Portovenere, Liguria. [12]
Spanish Pink. Rosa Valencia from Barxeta, Buscarro, Valencia. [12,16]
Victoria Red. Deep red form of Cork Red from Baneshane, Midleton, Co Cork. [7,8,9]

Varieties of Marble and Producing Countries

The above table lists 126 marbles to which should be added a further three which remain unidentified (See Part I – Identifying the Marbles). If, however, Acqua Bianca is included as White Carrara, Imperial Yellow as Portoro, Verde Cesana as Verde Alpi, Victoria Red as Cork Red, and the unidentified green marble outside St George's Chapel as Verde Antico, and if Blue and Grey Hymettian, Dark and Light Swedish Green, and Verde Antico Dark and Pale are amalgamated, the total becomes 121.

The marbles were obtained from quarries in the following countries: Algeria, Belgium, Brazil, Canada, Chile, Egypt, England, Finland, France, Greece, Ireland, Italy, Morocco, Norway, Portugal, Scotland, South Africa, Spain, Sweden, Switzerland, Tunisia, Turkey, USA and Yugoslavia (now Croatia). Source 8 lists the Lapis Lazuli in St Joseph's Chapel as from Badakhshan quarries, presumably those in the Kokcha River valley in the Badakhshan Province of Afghanistan. If this is correct the total number of countries is 25.

A crab set in Iona Green marble on the floor of St Andrew's Chapel.

Part VI – Notes

Numbered Sources are listed at the end of Part VII.

Note a: In geology, marble is the term for limestone which has been completely re-crystallised by heat and pressure. In decorative terms, as used here, it is simply a term to describe a stone which takes a polish. Thus granite, porphyry and alabaster, not normally regarded as marble, are included here. The term antico or antique denotes that the marble was used in antiquity, usually by the Romans.

Note b: Bianco del Mare (surround to the list of chief pastors in north aisle, arches in St Joseph's Chapel), Roman Stone (arches in west gallery and transepts) and Repen Zola (arches in Holy Souls Chapel and Crypt), are similar but distinct buff to grey marbles. Together with Hopton Wood Stone from Derbyshire (arches in Sanctuary, piscinas in St Paul's, holy water stoups) they are used for many of the Cathedral arches, frames and mouldings. Bianco del Mare comes from quarries near Split in Dalmatia, now part of Croatia. The others come from the border area between Italy and Yugoslavia around Trieste, attached to Italy in 1954, and Istria which was given by Italy to Yugoslavia in 1947 under the Treaty of Paris and is now also in Croatia.

Note c: Breccia Violetta (Brèche Violette or Violet Breccia) is quarried in the Seravezza area of Tuscany and is sometimes referred to as Breccia di Seravezza. It ranges from white with a few lilac stains (as on the floor of St Gregory and St Augustine's Chapel), through a more pronounced violet flushed marble (panels on nave balustrade and Lady Chapel walls), a strident purple (side porch walls and panels on baldacchino) to a deep black breccia (panels above columns on the south wall of St Patrick's Chapel).

Note d: Red or orange Brèche Sanguine (disk over exit to north west porch, large panels either side of 1st and 3rd gallery piers, St George's Chapel altar frontal), and Grande Brèche de Klaber (Holy Souls Chapel floor), come from quarries at Kleber (called Klaber by Source 1) in Algeria, which was renamed Sidi Ben Yekba after Algerian independence from France in 1962. Brèche Rose (tympanum above main entrance), Rose de Numidie (Blessed Sacrament Chapel walls) and pink-flushed Giallo Antico (Lady Chapel walls) also come from Kleber quarries. Sidi Ben Yekba is 16 miles north-east of Oran in Oran Province in north-west Algeria. A very similar variety of Giallo Antico comes from old Roman quarries at Chemtou in Tunisia.

Note e: The dark green breccia known as Brèche Universelle, Breccia Universale and Breccia Verde d'Egitto, though not identified as such at the time, is believed to have first been used in the Cathedral in 1908 by the firm of Farmer & Brindley for decorating the upper floor of the Lady Chapel. Farmer & Brindley are said to have held large slabs of Brèche Universelle in 1909 (Proceedings of the Geologists Association 21(3)09). Twenty years later the decoration of the west wall of St Patrick's Chapel by the same firm included a central panel of marble clearly cut from the same block and recorded as Brèche Universelle from the Nile (Cathedral Chronicle 9.28 and Source 19). In 1939 the decoration of the floor in St Joseph's Chapel by Fenning & Co of Hammersmith was said to include Breccia Universale (Chronicle 3.40), and in 1956 the firm's decoration of the lower floor of the Lady Chapel was reported to include Egyptian Breccia in the centre (Chronicle 11.56).

Note f: Source 1 lists the twin red granite entrance columns in the Narthex and the six red granite columns in the Crypt as Norwegian red granite. Norway's Geological Survey in Trondheim (Tom Heldal) states that Norway does not (and did not) produce red granite of this type. The Narthex columns appear to be Swedish Imperial Red granite from quarries 20 miles north of Oskarshamn, Kalmar; the Crypt granites Dark Shap from Cumbria, Carmen Red from 30 miles east of Kotka Koivunieni in Finland and, again, Imperial Red from Sweden. Twin columns of Dark Shap granite can also be found in the Cathedral Gift Shop. (Sources 12, 15, 19 and Norway's Geological Survey).

Note g: Norwegian Labradorite, as it is called by Source 1, is also known as Larvikite and comes from Larvik in Norway. Widely used in the Cathedral for column bases, chapel entrance steps and kerbs, with a column at the entrance to the Holy Souls Chapel and another in the Sacristy, its colour of grey to black with iridescent flecks of silver mica is distinctive.

Note h: Roman Pavonazzetto, named after its supposed resemblance to a peacock (pavone in Italian), came from Docimeion in what is now Turkey. This marble is no longer available and has been succeeded by Italian Pavonazzo from Seravezza in Tuscany, a variegated, cream coloured marble with deep purple veining (the Cathedral tribune columns). There is also pink flushed Pavonazzo from Seravezza (wall panels in the Lady Chapel apse), green veined Pavonazzo (the pulpit and south wall of the south transept) and blue veined Pavonazzo (colonnettes below the windows in St Paul's Chapel and either side of the altar in St George's). Both green and blue veined varieties come from Carrara. Source 1 states that the Pavonazzo columns for the Baptistry screen were quarried in Greece (no location given) and captured by the Turks while awaiting shipment with columns of Verde Antico at Larissa in Thessaly. The columns could conceivably be from Skyros but closely resemble a variety quarried at Carrara (Sample 346 at the Sedgwick Museum of Geology, Cambridge). (Sources 13, 14, 17).

Note i: The dark red panels of Rosso Laguna on the nave piers at gallery level were incorrectly described in the Westminster Cathedral Bulletin of June 1995 as from the Dolomite foothills north of Verona, when they were installed for the centenary of the Cathedral in 1995. They are in fact from near Bodrum in Turkey. Turkish marble is often exported through Italy and described as Italian for commercial reasons.

Note j: Source 4 describes the cream and purple main columns at both Transepts as from Brescia near Verona, Source 2 also as from near Verona, Source 3 as Tuscan. Source 1 describes them as 'from quarries near Verona between Pietro Santo and Serra Vezza.' Brescia is in Lombardy in Northern Italy, 35 miles from Verona. Seravezza is three miles from Pietrasanta in Tuscany, over a hundred miles to the south. Sources 16 and 19 state that the columns are of Breccia di Seravezza and this appears to be correct.

Note k: Yellow (Giallo) Siena is plain yellow of a rich, uniform tint (altar frontal in the Chapel of St Gregory and St Augustine). Pale (Chiaro) or Ivory (Avorio) Siena, sometimes also called 'Straw Siena', has a lighter, almost white in parts, ground colour without distinctive markings (floor in St Patrick's Chapel). Golden Siena is darker (disks above the doors in the Lady Chapel apse). Chocolate Siena is darker still, a purplish yellow, while Convent Siena (from the Convent of Montarrenti) is almost covered with dark blue or purple veins. Siena marble is quarried in the area of Montagnola Senese in the Siena region. (Sources 1, 7, 8, 9, 21).

Note I: There are at least three varieties of Verona marble in the Cathedral. Yellow Verona (Giallo Verona) was used for the eight great columns supporting the baldacchino over the high altar and for the columns either side of the altar in St Patrick's Chapel. Red Verona (Rosso Verona) can be seen high up at gallery level on either side of the main sanctuary and on the floor in front of the altar in the Chapel of St Gregory and St Augustine. Panels of lighter Red Verona, enclosed in Pink Verona (Rosato Verona) line the underside of the entrance arches to this chapel. All three varieties have the characteristic mottled appearance of Verona marble and are sometimes called Broccatello because of this. They are produced at quarries north of Verona, at Sant' Ambrogio, Valpolicella, Valpatena and in the Monte Baldo region beside Lake Garda. Verona marbles have been used extensively in Italy, particularly in the City of Verona, in Venice where they can be found decorating St Mark's Basilica and the Doge's Palace, and at the Lido where Red Verona is even used for paving slabs. (Sources 1, 13, 15, 16, 21).

A plinth of Vert d'Estours marble with a cross of Breccia Violetta in a Cathedral entrance porch.

PART VII

SOURCES

A block of Campan Rouge at the quarry.

PART VII – SOURCES

Part I - General

Marble in History: Pliny the Elder, 'Natural History', Book 36; Arthur Lee, 'Marble and Marble Workers', London, 1888; WR Lethaby and H Swainson, 'The Church of Sancta Sophia, Constantinople', Macmillan, 1894; William Brindley, 'Sancta Sophia, Constantinople and St Mark's, Venice', RIBA Journal, 1905; Mary Winearls Porter, 'What Rome was built with', London, 1907; Edward Hutton, 'The Cosmati', Routledge and Kegan Paul, 1950; Giorgio Vasari, 'Vasari on Technique', Dover, 1960; Angelina Dworakowska, 'Quarries in Ancient Greece', Wroclaw, 1975; Luciana and Tiziano Mannoni, 'Marble – The History of a Culture', Facts on File, 1985; J M Roberts, 'The Triumph of the West', London 1985; Marc Waelkens, Paul de Pape and Luc Moens, 'Quarries and the Marble Trade in Antiquity', Kluwer Academic Publishers, 1988; J B Ward-Perkins, 'Marble in Antiquity', British School at Rome, 1992; Yannis Maniatis, 'The Study of Marble and Other Stones used in Antiquity', Archetype, 1995; M Korres, 'From Pentelicon to the Parthenon', Melissa, Athens, 1995; Amanda Claridge, 'Oxford Archaeological Guides – Rome', OUP, 1998; Jacques Dubarry de Lassale, 'Identifying Marble', Editions H Vial, Paris, 2000.

The Marble Seekers: Kelly's London Post Office Directory (Streets, Commercial and Trades) entries for Farmer & Brindley 1863, 65, 68, 81, 83, 85, 87, 88, 96, 99, 1908, 24, 29; Charles Garnier, 'Le Nouvel Opera de Paris', Paris, 1878; R L Playfair, Blue Book of Consular Reports, (France, Algiers), 1881; R L Playfair, Proceedings of the British Association (Geological Section K), 1885; William Brindley, RIBA Transactions, 1887, 88, 94-95, 96-97, 1902-03, 07; 'The Builder', 12.5.1888, 20.9.90, 14.3.19 (Brindley obituary); 'The Building News', 11.4.1890; Lethaby and Swainson, 'The Church of Sancta Sophia, Constantinople', Macmillan 1894; 'The Quarry and Builders Merchant', Vol 44, 1899; 'Westminster Cathedral Record', 2.99; 'The Catholic Herald', 20.2.1903; Mary Winearls Porter, 'What Rome was built with', London, 1907; Proceedings of the Geologists Association, 21(3)1909; W G Renwick, 'Marble and Marble Working', London, 1909; Will of William Brindley, 2.6.1919; Winefride de l'Hôpital, 'Westminster Cathedral and its Architect', Hutchinson, 1919; 'Westminster Cathedral Chronicle', 10.19, 1.22, 3.24, 9.28, 9.30, 1.31, 9.35, 3.56, 11.56, 6.57, 9.59, 10.59, 12.60, 5.63, 8.63, 7.64; Farmer & Brindley Company Records, 1929; Edward Hutton, 'An Unknown Victorian', The Nineteenth Century and After, Vol CXV, 1.1934; Records of the Advisory Committee for the Decoration of Westminster Cathedral, 1939-42 and 1954-61; Letters between Mary Winearls Porter and Francis Bartlett, 13.1.65, 21.1.65, 2.2.65; Angelina Dworakowska, 'Quarries in Ancient Greece', Wroclaw, 1975; Stephen Bayley 'The Albert Memorial', Scolar Press 1981; Benedict Read, 'Victorian Sculpture', Yale, 1982; 'Royal Commission on Historical Monuments of England – County Hall', Athlone, 1991; Emma Hardy, 'Farmer & Brindley', Victorian Society Annual, 1993; M Korres, 'From Pentelicon to the Parthenon', Melissa, Athens, 1995; Opera National de Paris, 'Visite de l'Opera Palais Garnier'; Farmer & Brindley references in Nikolaus Pevsner et al 'The Buildings of England' series; Cathedral architectural drawings B-23, 25, 28, 31, 40, C-8, 11, 50, 52, 55, D-5, 9, 16, 68, 83, 88, F-65, H-4, 15.

Identifying the Marbles: G H Blagrove, 'Marble Decoration and the Terminology of British and Foreign Marbles', London, 1888; W G Renwick, 'Marble and Marble Working', London, 1909; 'The Builder', 10.12.1915; John Watson, 'British and Foreign Marbles and Other Ornamental Stones', Cambridge, 1916; 'Winefride de l'Hôpital', 'Westminster Cathedral and its Architect', Hutchinson, 1919; Mario Catello, 'Il Piemonte Marmifero', Turin, 1929; G M Davies, 'The Geology of London and South-East England', Chapter 16, Thomas Murby, 1939; M Grant, 'The Marbles and Granites of the World', London, 1955; Francis Bartlett, Annotated Photographs of the Cathedral, 1954-56; Letters between Mary Winearls Porter and Francis Bartlett, 13.1.65, 21.1.65, 2.2.65; 'Westminster Cathedral Record', 1896-1902; 'Westminster Cathedral Chronicle', 1907-67; Francis Bartlett, Westminster Cathedral Friends Newsletters, Spring and Autumn 1989; Architectural Plans and Drawings of the Cathedral; 'Royal Commission on Historical Monuments of England – County Hall', Athlone Press, 1991; 'TRE Annual Lapidei 1996, 1997', Conegliano, Italy; International Italmarmi SRL, Massa, Carrara, Italy; Information from: Mrs Pia Bruno Allasio, Mondovi, Cuneo, Italy, 1996-2000; Prof Vanni Badino, Turin University Mining Department, Piedmont, Italy, 2000; Aelred Bartlett, 2000-2; Jacques Dubarry de Lassale, 'Identifying Marble', Editions H Vial, Paris, 2000; Information from: Department of Mineralogy, Natural History Museum, London; Oxford University Museum of Natural History; Sedgwick Museum of Geology, Cambridge; Trinity College Museum, Dublin; Office of Public Works, 51 St Stephen's Green, Dublin; Gerald Culliford, Gerald Culliford Ltd, Kingston, Surrey; Ian Macdonald, McMarmilloyd Ltd, Great Bedwyn, Wiltshire.

Part II – The Main Cathedral Marbles and their History

A Tour of the Marbles: 'Westminster Cathedral Record' (Supplement to The Tablet), 29.12.1900; John Watson, 'British and Foreign Marbles and Other Ornamental Stones', Cambridge, 1916; Winefride de l'Hôpital, 'Westminster Cathedral and its Architect', Hutchinson, 1919; 'Westminster Cathedral Chronicle'; Francis Bartlett, Annotated Photographs of the Cathedral, 1954-56; Francis Bartlett, Westminster Cathedral Friends Newsletters, Spring and Autumn 1989; J B Ward-Perkins, 'Marble in Antiquity', British School at Rome, 1992; 'Westminster Cathedral Bulletin', 5.95, 6.95; 'Oremus', 11.2000; Cathedral architectural drawings; Information from Gerald Culliford of Gerald Culliford Ltd, Ian MacDonald of McMarmilloyd Ltd, Henry Buckley and Dave Smith of the Natural History Museum in London, Monica Price of The University Museum of Natural History at Oxford and Tom Heldal of Norway's Geological Survey, Trondheim.

The Lost Columns: John Ruskin, 'The Stones of Venice', Dent, 1851; 'Westminster Cathedral Record', 2.99; 'The Tablet', 13.5.99, 29.12.1900, 7.6.02; Winefride de l'Hôpital, 'Westminster Cathedral and its Architect', Hutchinson, 1919; Henry Tristram, 'Cardinal Newman and the Church of Birmingham Oratory', Birmingham, 1934; Shane Leslie, 'Letters of Herbert Cardinal Vaughan to Lady Herbert of Lea', Burns & Oates, 1942; 'Westminster Cathedral Chronicle', 5.49; Paul Chavasse, 'The Birmingham Oratory Church'; Cathedral architectural drawing F-65.

Verde Antico: William Brindley, RIBA Transactions 1887, 94-95, 96-97, 1907; Lethaby and Swainson, 'The Church of Sancta Sophia, Constantinople', Macmillan, 1894; Kelly's London Post Office Directory (Trades), 1896, 1907, 1913; 'Illustrated London News', 24.4.1897 - 11.6.98; 'Westminster Cathedral Record', 2.99; 'The Tablet', 13.5.99, 29.12.1900; A Cordella, 'The Marbles of Greece', Stone Magazine, Vol XXIV No. 1, 1902; British Consular Report, 'More about the Grecian Marbles', Stone Magazine, Vol XXIV No. 5, 1902; Mary Winearls Porter, 'What Rome was built with', London, 1907; W G Renwick, 'Marble and Marble Working', London, 1909; John Watson, 'British and Foreign Marbles and Other Ornamental Stones', Cambridge, 1916; Winefride de l'Hôpital, 'Westminster Cathedral and its Architect', Hutchinson, 1919; 'Westminster Cathedral Chronicle', 4.32, 5.63, 8.63, 7.64; Angelina Dworakowska, 'Quarries in Ancient Greece', Wroclaw, 1975; J B Ward-Perkins, 'Marble in Antiquity', British School at Rome, 1992; Zane Katsikis, 'Greece by Rail', Bradt 1997; Information from Tsalmas Melas of Tsalmas Marmi/Tsalma Marble, Larissa, May 2000, May 2003; Field Trip to Larissa and Verde Antico quarries below Mount Ossa, May 2003, September 2004.

Rosso Antico: RIBA Transactions, 1869; 'The Times' (Byron Memorial) 27.5.1880, 8.12.1880; Farmer & Brindley in Kelly's London Post Office Directory (Commercial and Trades) 1887, 1899, 1908, 1923; A Cordella, 'The Marbles of Greece', Stone Magazine, Vol XXIV No. 1, 1902; British Consular Report, 'More about the Grecian Marbles', Stone Magazine, Vol XXIV No. 5, 1902; W G Renwick, 'Marble and Marble Working', London, 1909; 'Westminster Cathedral Chronicle', 12.60; Angelina Dworakowska, 'Quarries in Ancient Greece', Wroclaw, 1975; Frederick Cooper, 'The Quarries of Mount Taygetos in the Peloponnesos, Greece', in Herz and Waelkens 'Classical Marble: Geochemistry, Technology, Trade', Kluwer Academic Publishers, 1988; Lorenzo Lazzarini, 'Rosso Antico and other Red Marbles used in Antiquity', J Paul Getty Museum, Malibu, Ca. 1990; J B Ward-Perkins, 'Marble in Antiquity', British School at Rome, 1992; Gabriele Borghini, 'Marmi Antichi', Edizioni De Luca, Rome, 1998; Matthias Bruno, 'Mianes, Cape Tenaron: A new quarry of green Cipollino and of red Fior de Pesco, Asmosia 5, Archetype 2002; Field Trip to Paganea, Cape Tenaro and Profitis Ilias quarries, May 2000, April 2005, April 2008.

Cipollino: Pliny the Elder, 'Natural History' Book 36; Charles Garnier, 'Le Nouvel Opera de Paris', Paris, 1878; Farmer & Brindley in Kelly's London Post Office Directory (Trades) 1881, 85, 99, 1908; William Brindley, RIBA Transactions, 1887, 94-95, 1907; Lethaby and Swainson, 'The Church of Sancta Sophia, Constantinople', Macmillan, 1894; 'Westminster Cathedral Record', 2.99; 'The Tablet', 13.5.99, 29.12.1900; William Brindley, 'The Ancient Marble Quarries of Greek Cipollino', Stone Magazine, Vol XVIII No. 2, 1899; Farmer & Brindley Company Records, 1905; Mary Winearls Porter, 'What Rome was built with', London, 1907; W G Renwick, 'Marble and Marble Working', London, 1909; John Watson, 'British and Foreign Marbles and Other Ornamental Stones', Cambridge, 1916; Winefride de l'Hôpital, 'Westminster Cathedral and its Architect', Hutchinson, 1919; 'Westminster Cathedral Chronicle', 3.56, 9/10.59, 12.60; Angelina Dworakowska, 'Quarries in Ancient Greece', Wroclaw, 1975; J B Ward-Perkins, 'Marble in Antiquity', British School at Rome, 1992; Yannis Maniatis, 'The Study of Marble and other Stones used in Antiquity', Archetype, 1995; Information from Aelred Bartlett 2000-2; Field Trip to Karystos and Kylindroi Quarry on Mount Ochi, May 2003.

White Pentelic: William Brindley, 'Marble: Its Uses as Suggested by the Past', RIBA Transactions, 1887; A Cordella, 'The Marbles of Greece', Stone Magazine, Vol XXIV No.1, 1902; British Consular Report, 'More about the Grecian Marbles', Stone Magazine, Vol XXIV No. 5, 1902; Mary Winearls Porter, 'What Rome was built with', London, 1907; 'Westminster Cathedral Chronicle', 5.07, 6.07, 7.07, 4.08, 2.10, 6.10, 6.11, 7.11, 5.63; W G Renwick, 'Marble and Marble Working', London, 1909; John Watson, 'British and Foreign Marbles and Other Ornamental Stones', Cambridge, 1916; Winefride de l'Hôpital, 'Westminster Cathedral and its Architect', Hutchinson, 1919; J B Ward-Perkins, 'Marble in Antiquity', British School at Rome, 1992; M Korres, 'From Pentelicon to the Parthenon', Melissa, Athens, 1995; Field Trip to Athens and Mount Pentelicon quarries, May 2003.

Green Porphyry: Pliny the Elder, 'Natural History', Book 36; Strabo, 'Geography', Book 8 Chapter 5; Lethaby and Swainson, 'The Church of Sancta Sophia, Constantinople', Macmillan, 1894; Mary Winearls Porter, 'What Rome was built with', London, 1907; John Watson, 'British and Foreign Marbles and Other Ornamental Stones', Cambridge, 1916; Winefride de l'Hôpital, 'Westminster Cathedral and its Architect', Hutchinson, 1919; Edward Hutton, 'The Cosmati', Routledge and Kegan Paul, 1950; Raniero Gnoli, 'Marmora Romana', Rome, 1971; Angelina Dworakowska, 'Quarries in Ancient Greece', Wroclaw, 1975; J B Ward-Perkins, 'Marble in Antiquity', British School at Rome, 1992; Peter Warren, 'Lapis Lacedaemonius', British School at Athens, 1992; Patrizio Pensabene, 'Il Marmo et il Colore', Rome, 1998; Gabriele Borghini, 'Marmi Antichi', Edizioni De Luca, Rome, 1998; Patrizio Pensabene, 'I Marmi Colorati della Roma Imperiale', Marsilio, 2002; Field Trip to Stephania and Green Porphyry quarry, April 2005, April 2008.

Purple Porphyry: Pliny the Elder, 'Natural History', Book 36; William Brindley, RIBA Transactions 1887, 88, 1907; 'The Builder', 12.11.1887, 20.9.90; Farmer & Brindley in Kelly's London Post Office Directory (Trades) 1888, 1908; Lethaby and Swainson, 'The Church of Sancta Sophia, Constantinople', Macmillan, 1894; Mary Winearls Porter, 'What Rome was built with', London, 1907; John Watson, 'British and Foreign Marbles and Other Ornamental Stones', Cambridge, 1916; 'Westminster Cathedral Chronicle', 9.28; David Meredith, 'The Journal of Egyptian Archaeology', 1952; Giorgio Vasari, 'Vasari on Technique', Dover 1960; F G B Millar, 'Condemnation to Hard Labour in the Roman Empire', British School at Rome, 1984; J B Ward-Perkins, 'Marble in Antiquity', British School at Rome, 1992; Stephen Bann, 'The Sculpture of Stephen Cox', 1995; Suzanne Butters, 'The Triumph of Vulcan', Leo S Olschki, 1996; 21st Century British Sculpture 'Stephen Cox', 2002. 'Current World Archaeology', No 8, 11/12, 2004; Field Trip to Mons Claudianus and Mons Porphyrites quarries, November 2006.

Carrara: Pliny the Elder, 'Natural History', Book 36; Arthur Lee, 'Marble and Marble Workers', London, 1888; Mary Winearls Porter, 'What Rome was built with', London, 1907; W G Renwick, 'Marble and Marble Working', London, 1909; John Watson, 'British and Foreign Marbles and Other Ornamental Stones', Cambridge, 1916; Winefride de l'Hôpital, 'Westminster Cathedral and its Architect', Hutchinson, 1919; Giorgio Vasari, 'Vasari on Technique', Dover, 1960; Cathy Newman, 'Carrara Marble', National Geographic, 7.82; Luciana and Tiziano Mannoni, 'Marble - The History of a Culture', Facts on File Publications, 1985; J B Ward-Perkins, 'Marble in Antiquity', British School at Rome, 1992; Yannis Maniatis, 'The Study of Marble and other Stones used in Antiquity', Archetype, 1995; 'TRE Annual Lapidei 1997', Conegliano, Italy; Field Trip to Carrara, Fantiscritti and Monte Altissimo quarries, September 2000, May 2004.

Portoro: John Watson, 'British and Foreign Marbles and Other Ornamental Stones', Cambridge, 1916; Winefride de L'Hôpital, 'Westminster Cathedral and its Architect', Hutchinson, 1919; Giorgio Vasari, 'Vasari on Technique', Dover, 1960; Raniero Gnoli, 'Marmora Romana', Rome, 1971; Cathedral architectural drawings; Field Trip to Portovenere and Portoro quarries, May 2004.

Grand Antique des Pyrénées: C P Brard, 'Traité des Pierres Précieuses, des Porphyres, Granits, Marbres, Albâtres et Autres Roches', Paris, 1808; G H Blagrove, 'Marble Decoration and the Terminology of British and Foreign Marbles', London, 1888; Arthur Lee, 'Marble and Marble Workers', London, 1888; Lethaby and Swainson, 'The Church of Sancta Sophia, Constantinople', Macmillan, 1894; Mary Winearls Porter, 'What Rome was built with', London, 1907; John Watson, 'British and Foreign Marbles and Other Ornamental Stones', Cambridge, 1916; Winefride de l'Hôpital, 'Westminster Cathedral and its Architect', Hutchinson, 1919; 'Westminster Cathedral Chronicle', 12.60; Raniero Gnoli, 'Marmora Romana', Rome, 1971; Susanna Van Rose, 'Marbles of the French Pyrenees', 1991; J B Ward-Perkins, 'Marble in Antiquity', British School at Rome, 1992; Gabriele Borghini, 'Marmi Antichi', Edizioni De Luca, Rome, 1998; Patrizio Pensabene, 'Il Marmo et il Colore', Rome, 1998; Jacques Dubarry de Lassale, 'Identifying Marble', Editions H Vial, Paris, 2000; Field Trip to Aubert and Grand Antique quarry, August 2003, July 2007.

Campan: C P Brard, 'Traité des Pierres Précieuses, des Porphyres, Granits, Marbres, Albâtres, et Autres Roches', Paris, 1888; G H Blagrove, 'Marble Decoration and the Terminology of British and Foreign Marbles', London, 1888; W G Renwick, 'Marble and Marble Working', London, 1909; John Watson, 'British and Foreign Marbles and Other Ornamental Stones', Cambridge, 1916; Winefride de l'Hôpital, 'Westminster Cathedral and its Architect', Hutchinson, 1919; Raniero Gnoli, 'Marmora Romana', Rome, 1971; 'Nomenclature des Carrières Françaises de Roches', Le Mausolée, 1976; J B Ward-Perkins, 'Marble in Antiquity', British School at Rome, 1992; Gabriele Borghini, 'Marmi Antichi', Edizioni De Luca, Rome, 1998; Patrizio Pensabene, 'Il Marmo et il Colore', Rome, 1998; Amanda Claridge, 'Oxford Archaeological Guides – Rome', OUP, 1998; Jacques Dubarry de Lassale, 'Identifying Marble', Editions H Vial, Paris, 2000; Information from Gerald Culliford of Gerald Culliford Ltd and Ian Macdonald of McMarmilloyd Ltd, 2006; Field Trip to Espiadet and the Campan quarry, July 2006.

Connemara Green: Mr and Mrs S C Hall, 'Ireland' (Pages 462-4), Hall, Virtue and Co, London, 1843; Henry Kinahan, 'Economic Geology of Ireland', RGSI, 1886-7; John Watson, 'British and Foreign Marbles and Other Ornamental Stones', Cambridge, 1916; Winefride de l'Hôpital, 'Westminster Cathedral and its Architect', Hutchinson, 1919; Michael Max, 'Connemara Marble and the Industry based upon it', GSI, 1985; E Naughton, 'The Assessment of Connemara Marble Resources', 1992; Kathleen Villiers-Tuthill, 'The History of Clifden', 1992; Patrick Wyse Jackson, 'The Building Stones of Dublin', Country House, 1993; 'Directory of Active Quarries, Pits and Mines in Ireland', GSI, 1994; Connemara Marble Industries Brochures; Information from Ambrose Joyce (father and son), Moycullen, Co Galway, and Mark Joyce, Recess, Co Galway, June 2002; Field Trip to Streamstown, Barnanoraun and Lissoughter quarries, June 2002, May 2007.

Cork Red: Henry Kinahan 'Economic Geology of Ireland', RGSI, 1886-7; John Watson, 'British and Foreign Marbles and Other Ornamental Stones', Cambridge, 1916; Winefride de l'Hôpital, 'Westminster Cathedral and its Architect', Hutchinson, 1919; W E Nevill, Geological Magazine, 12.12.62; Patrick Wyse Jackson, 'The Building Stones of Dublin', Country House, 1993; Geological Survey of Ireland (GSI), MinLocs Database and Maps; GSI Mineral Resources Research Unit - Site Report (Baneshane), 28.3.88; A G Sleeman, 'Geology of South Cork'; Colin Rynne, 'The Industrial Archaeology of Cork City and its Environs'; 'The Sunday Telegraph', 22.1.95; Information from Maighread Hyde, Midleton, Co Cork and Aelred Bartlett, 2000-2; Field Trip to Baneshane, Midleton and Little Island quarries, April 2002.

Kilkenny Black: 'A Tour of Ireland', By Two Englishmen, London, 1748; William Tighe, 'Statistical Survey of the County of Kilkenny', Dublin, 1802; Mr and Mrs S C Hall, 'Ireland' (Pages 40-41), Hall, Virtue and Company, London, 1843; Edward Hull, 'On Building and Other Ornamental Stones', Macmillan, 1872; Henry Kinahan, 'Economic Geology of Ireland', RGSI, 1886-7; Arthur Lee, 'Marble and Marble Workers', London, 1888; John Watson, 'British and Foreign Marbles and Other Ornamental Stones', Cambridge, 1916; Winefride de l'Hôpital, 'Westminster Cathedral and its Architect', Hutchinson, 1919; 'Westminster Cathedral Chronicle', 9.28; J C J Murphy, 'The Kilkenny Marble Works', Old Kilkenny Review, 1948; Patrick Wyse Jackson, 'The Building Stones of Dublin', Country House, 1993; Geological Survey Maps of County Kilkenny, GSI, Dublin; Field Trip to the Black Quarry, Butler's Quay Quarry and Colles's Marble Sawing Mill, April 2006.

Iona Green: 'The Builder', 10.12.1915; 'Westminster Cathedral Chronicle' 12.1915; Winefride de l'Hôpital, 'Westminster Cathedral and its Architect', Hutchinson, 1919; E M MacArthur, 'Iona, 1750-1914', 1990; David Viner, 'The Iona Marble Quarry', New Iona Press, 1992; Anna Ritchie, 'Historic Scotland - Iona', 1997; Field Trip to Iona marble quarry, July 1997, August 1998, July 2002.

Derbyshire Fossil and Hopton Wood: Arthur Lee, 'Marble and Marble Workers', London, 1888; W G Renwick, 'Marble and Marble Working', London, 1909; John Watson, 'British and Foreign Marbles and Other Ornamental Stones', Cambridge, 1916; 'Westminster Cathedral Chronicle', 7.18, 5.26, 4.29; Winefride de l'Hôpital, 'Westminster Cathedral and its Architect', Hutchinson, 1919; Malcolm Yorke, 'Eric Gill, Man of Flesh and Spirit', Constable, 1981; John Browne and Tim Dean, 'Westminster Cathedral: Building of Faith', Booth-Clibborn, 1995; Ian Thomas, 'Tarmac's Derbyshire Heritage', The Tarmac Papers, 2000; Cathedral architectural drawings; Information from Ian Thomas, Director of the National Stone Centre, and Francis Lowe of Francis N Lowe Ltd, Middleton, Derbyshire; Field Trip to Coalhills, Steeplehouse and Dene quarries, November 2001, July 2007.

Gerontius and Princess Blue: 'The Tablet', 13.6.1903, 2.5.1903; Proceedings of the Geologists Association, 21(3)1909; W G Renwick, 'Marble and Marble Working', London, 1909; John Watson, 'British and Foreign Marbles and Other Ornamental Stones', Cambridge, 1916; Winefride de l'Hôpital, 'Westminster Cathedral and its Architect', Hutchinson, 1919; 'Oremus', 11.2003; Information from McMarmilloyd Ltd and Taylor Pearce Ltd, 2004.

SOURCES REFERRED TO BY NUMBER IN PARTS IV, V AND VI

1. Winefride de l'Hôpital, 'Westminster Cathedral and its Architect', Hutchinson, 1919.

2. Francis Bartlett, Westminster Cathedral Friends Newsletters, Spring and Autumn 1989.

3. Francis Bartlett, Annotated Photographs of the Cathedral, 1954-56.

4. 'Westminster Cathedral Record', 1896-1902; 'Westminster Cathedral Chronicle', 1907-67.

5. Westminster Cathedral Architectural Plans and Drawings.

6. G H Blagrove, 'Marble Decoration and the Terminology of British and Foreign Marbles', London, 1888.

7. W G Renwick, 'Marble and Marble Working', London, 1909.

8. J Watson, 'British and Foreign Marbles and Other Ornamental Stones', Cambridge, 1916.

9. M Grant, 'The Marbles and Granites of the World', London, 1955.

10. Istituto Commercio Estero, 'Marmi Italiani', 1982.

11. Marble Institute of America, 'A list of The World's Marbles', 1990.

12. Department of Mineralogy, Natural History Museum, London.

13. Oxford University Museum of Natural History, Oxford.

14. Sedgwick Museum of Geology, Cambridge.

15. Gerald Culliford, Gerald Culliford Ltd, Kingston, Surrey.

16. Ian Macdonald, McMarmilloyd Ltd, Great Bedwyn, Wiltshire.

17. Prof Lorenzo Lazzarini, University of Venice, Italy.

18. Prof Vanni Badino, Mining Department, University of Turin, Italy.

19. G M Davies, 'The Geology of London and South-East England', Chapter XVI 'The Stones of London - Westminster Cathedral', Thomas Murby, 1939.

20. T Dean and J Browne, 'Westminster Cathedral: Building of Faith', Booth-Clibborn, 1995.

21. 'TRE Annual Lapidei', 1996, 1997, 2000, 2001, Conegliano, Italy.

22. Jacques Dubarry de Lassale, 'Identifying Marble', Editions H Vial, Paris, 2000.